Cycling in & around Birmingham

Philip Routledge

Published by Sigma Leisure – an imprint of
Sigma Press, 1 South Oak Lane, Wilmslow. Cheshire SK9 6AR, England.

British Library Cataloguing in Publication Data
A CIP record for this book is available from the British Library.

ISBN: 1-85058-498-2

Typesetting and Design by: Sigma Press, Wilmslow, Cheshire.

Cover photograph: Dimmingsdale Bridge, on the Staffordshire & Worcestershire canal

Maps and photographs: the author

Printed by: MFP Design and Print

Preface

I have carefully prepared this book to guide you to the very best leisure cycling opportunities in the Birmingham area and offer you an immense variation of landscape, townscape and dedicated cycle routes. It will show you the best way to begin an exploration of the area, and give clear directions and descriptions of the individual routes and surrounding locations. I take the view that leisure cycling is an unstressed activity, good exercise, a family pastime and a relaxed form of outdoor activity. These routes are not supposed to be challenging long-distance tours, they are designed with the considerations of family and leisure cycling as a priority. Some of the routes offer longer rides, some simply describe a first class cycling venue (often with children in mind), while others offer alternatives and possible extensions. For anybody who prefers a long ride, I have included my version of a full circuit route around Birmingham. This has been exactingly planned to incorporate as many major points of interest as possible and reflects the real Birmingham character by utilizing long stretches of canal towing-path.

Within reason, all of these rides are designed to achieve avoidance of traffic and unnecessary hill climbs. As a result of this philosophy, all of the rides are very user-friendly and can be enjoyed by anyone who can ride a bike, from the raw novice to the super fit sports rider. Each route is guaranteed to produce a worthwhile return for the effort put in by the rider and should offer a memorable and enjoyable experience.

With all of these excursions, as well as enjoying a pleasant cycle ride and some healthy exercise, the cyclist will draw equal satisfaction from some other aspect of the ride. This may be a surprising oasis of peace in a busy city environment, an industrial archaeological connection, a look at some rare wildlife, a different view of suburbia, an educational tour around Shakespeare country or simply some particularly interesting or attractive views or surroundings. Happy cycling!

Philip Routledge.

Contents

Introduction

The Rides

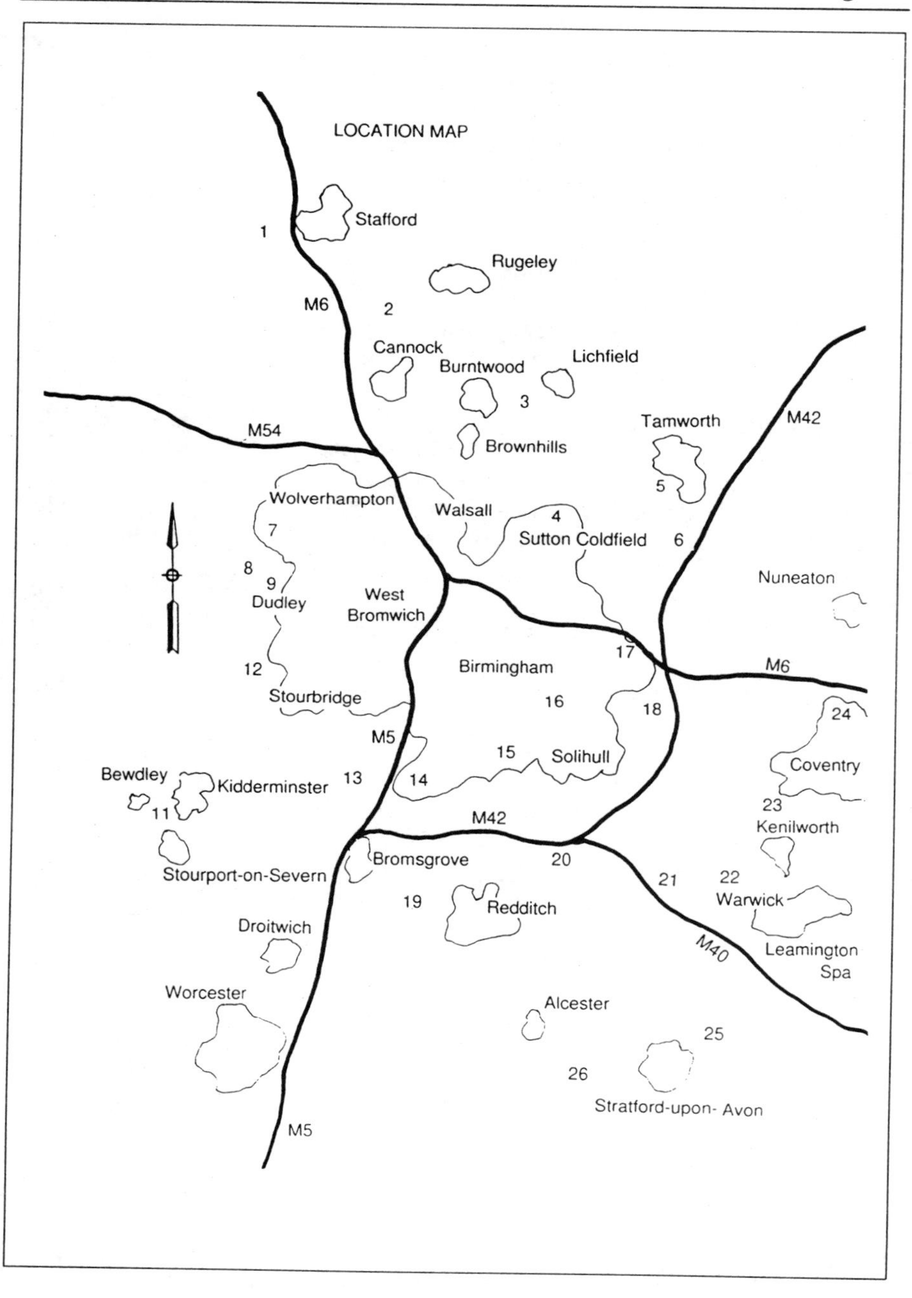
LOCATION MAP
Stafford
1
Rugeley
M6
2
Cannock
Burntwood
Lichfield
3
M54
Brownhills
Tamworth
M42
5
Wolverhampton
Walsall
4
Sutton Coldfield
6
7
8
9
Dudley
West
Bromwich
Nuneaton
17
M6
Birmingham
12
Stourbridge
16
18
24
M5
15
Solihull
Coventry
Bewdley
Kidderminster
13
14
11
23
M42
Kenilworth
Bromsgrove
20
21
22
Stourport-on-Severn
19
Redditch
Warwick
Droitwich
M40
Leamington
Spa
Worcester
Alcester
25
26
Stratford-upon- Avon
M5

Introduction

Birmingham and its surrounding rural area have more great cycling opportunities than most people would imagine. The three basic elements of good leisure cycling are: the avoidance of traffic and main roads, the avoidance of hills and bad ground and the addition of an interesting focal point or theme as a diversion to the effort of pedalling. These three elements have been of paramount importance in devising each of these fascinating routes.

If the idea of gently cycling along mile upon mile of quiet country lanes appeals to you, you need look no further. Discover the best places to go around Birmingham and the most interesting ways to reach them. Cycling is undoubtedly one of the very best ways to explore canals and there are plenty of towing-path routes included. If the prospect of cycling in a forest appeals, you don't need to travel to Scotland or North Wales but just to the edge of Birmingham. Head for Cannock or Wyre forest and find out just how pleasant these environments are. If you're looking for a place to let the children roam freely but safely with their bikes or if you want some fresh air and a little light exercise, try Kingsbury Water Park, Sutton Park or Babbs Lake. You may be surprised just how much fun these places can be. The rest is up to you. Get on your bike and enjoy yourself.

Equipment

- ☐ Additional equipment translates to additional weight.
- ☐ Additional weight translates to additional effort.
- ☐ Hills, especially upward hills, and head winds magnify the undesirable effects of additional weight.

Bearing these simple rules in mind, and on the assumption that your bike has pedals, wheels and security equipment, there are really only a few simple accessories that are worth considering. These are as follows:

The **bell** might well be fitted to your bike anyway. If it isn't, don't worry. You can always sing, cough or loudly clear your throat, but a bell is easier. It is associated with cycling and it is inoffensive.

The **frame corner pack** is useful because it is dedicated to carrying your **puncture kit, basic tool kit** and **first aid equipment**. Once it is packed, you can forget about it, but it will be there when needed. Keep the tools to a minimum. On most bikes two Allen keys, a multi spanner and a cross head screw driver are sufficient.

Your puncture repair kit is not much use without **a pump**.

A back (or front) rack is one of the most useful accessories you are likely to acquire for your bike. Once you've fitted one, you will wonder how you ever managed without.

Panniers, in either single or double form, enable you to carry spare clothing, sandwiches, cool drinks, and anything else which you may require.

A front mud/spray deflector or mudguard. You'll know why you need a front spray deflector the first time you try to ride without one on a wet or muddy surface.

Security

If you are leaving your bike out of sight, particularly in and around a large conurbation such as Birmingham, **lock it** or you will almost certainly have it stolen. It is a sad state of affairs, but according to crime prevention statistics, the chances of an unguarded and unlocked bicycle being stolen in a busy built-up area would be greater than 60% over a 48 hour period. The chances of a locked but unguarded bicycle being vandalised or having pieces taken off it, (such as wheels!) during periods of darkness are also very high. In simple terms, you are more likely to have your bicycle stolen than not have it stolen.

Use a **D-lock** around the frame, through the rear wheel and onto the most solid object you can find. Many local authorities and private organisations have gone to a great deal of expense and trouble to create proper cycle parking arrangements. Most commonly these are Sheffield Stands, strong n-shaped metal stands which are specially designed for bicycle locking. If possible, secure your front wheel, even if it means carrying two separate locking devices.

Make sure that you have a **photograph** of your bicycle and a note of any **serial numbers** or distinctive markings and carry this with you. Use special ultra-violet markers and write your name or post code on the bike. By doing this and having the descriptive information readily available, at least you can give the police a chance.

Just in case the worst does happen, always make sure you are carrying your bus fare to get home. A long walk after the indignation of losing your bike will dim even the brightest spirit.

Datatag is a high-tech method of protecting your bicycle against theft. As well as etching the frame with non removable and indelible warning labels, various electronic tagging devices are hidden around the frame and stems. Police forces are issued with detection devices which can read data from the electronic tags. A central computer keeps a record of the owner's name and address, thus creating a method of detecting stolen bikes and returning them to their rightful owners.

Safety

- ☐ Keep off the roads whenever possible.
- ☐ Be safe, be seen – lights at night, fluorescents by day.
- ☐ Ring your bell when approaching pedestrians.
- ☐ Wear helmets for rough, off-road riding.
- ☐ Make sure that your bicycle is properly maintained.

Traffic

The real joy of leisure cycling is the joy of riding along a quite lane, a canal towing-path or a dedicated cycle path in complete safety and without the fumes and noise of traffic.

Some experienced cyclists seem to have developed an immunity to the terrors of riding along busy main roads with their blind backs exposed and only inches from an endless stream of potentially lethal, fast-moving vehicles. Cyclists have a perfect right to use any road apart from motorways, and in certain cases adult cyclists may be obliged to use busy routes – for commuting, for instance. But for leisure cycling – why should you take any risks or expose yourself to any danger? You simply do not have to compete with traffic. The most important criterion in all of the routes in this book is the avoidance of heavy, fast-moving traffic wherever reasonably possible.

Buying a Bicycle

Apart from colour and budget, there are a few main deciding factors when buying a bicycle and these notes offer a few tips. Each type of bicycle has its own particular advantages and disadvantages. Here is a brief list of the major options along with the pros and cons of various categories.

Mountain Bike (also known as MTB or all- terrain bike – ATB)
Pro: Go anywhere. Very easy to ride, very manoeuverable.
Con: Poor for long-distance touring or speed work.

Roadster (traditionally, the vicar's bike)
Pro: Solid, hub gears. Will probably last for ever.
Con: Heavy and very hard to pedal up hill – which is probably why vicars are usually seen pushing.

Shopper (small-wheeled, lightweight bicycle. Mainly used by women)
Pro: Easy to ride, easy to store. Hardly ever stolen.
Con: No good off-road, not really for serious touring.

Folding bike
Pro: Transportable in tiny spaces such as car boots, canal boats, buses or trains. Great for the urban jungle. Modern designs have put the better versions on a par with traditional bikes.
Con: Usually not suitable for off-road or touring

Quality touring bicycle (often seen loaded with panniers)
Pro: A quality touring bicycle is a joy to ride and a joy to own. Long-distance riding can be carried out in comfort. The best all-round bicycle to own.
Con: Quality does not come cheap and really rough stuff should be left to the ATBs.

Hybrid (half mountain bike, half tourer)

Pro: Lighter and more comfortable than a mountain bike. Better on tarmac.
Con: Difficult to think of many drawbacks. Limited off-road ability.

Sporting bicycle (thin-rimmed wheels, drop bars)
Pro: Faster than a tourer.
Con: Not as comfortable or as strong as a tourer. Horrible on anything but billiard table surfaces.

Road racing bicycles (thin-rimmed wheels, quality lightweight frames)
Pro: Ultimate speed depends how much you are willing to pay. Expensive, specialist racing bicycles are a beauty to behold.
Con: Except for racing or training for racing, these machines are useless.

Owning a Bicycle

Owning a bicycle should be a great pleasure and a good bicycle, if well-maintained, will prove to be a friend for life. As with most things, ownership of a bicycle can be as expensive or as cheap as you care to make it.

Service Schedules: If you are using your bicycle regularly and you are not confident in carrying out your own servicing, an annual service at a reputable cycle dealer is a great investment.

Insurance: This is very much a matter of personal choice and personal circumstance. It is not compulsory and often you will be buying cover that you already have in another form. If you have one, check the terms of your home contents insurance policy and look into the possibility of paying a small extra premium for your cycling needs.

Cleaning: By cleaning your bicycle regularly you will achieve three things. Firstly, it will look better; secondly, it will operate more smoothly and thirdly, you will become aware of faults before they develop into serious problems. Use warm, soapy water and be certain to oil the chain and gears after the water has dried off. Wash carefully around the brakes and around the gear sets.

The Cyclist's Essential Check List

It is good practice to carry out the following quick checks each time you set out.

- ☐ **Tyres.** Inflated, good tread.
- ☐ **Tools.** Basic appropriate tools carried plus the pump.
- ☐ **Adjustments.** Are the saddle and the handlebars set at the correct height and rake?
- ☐ **Spare tube** and puncture repair kit.
- ☐ **Security.** D-lock or good chain carried.
- ☐ **Lubrication.** The chain should be oiled every fifty miles, after washing or rain or every two weeks when in use.
- ☐ **Lights.** Will you need them?
- ☐ **Food** and water if required.
- ☐ **Clothing.** Check the weather.
- ☐ **Condition of the bicycle.** A final look over your bicycle. Check your steering, brakes and gears.

Insects, sun, wind and rain

Insects: The use of a good insect repellent is an essential requirement, especially on hot summer days.

Sun: Take the appropriate precautions of sun protection cream.

Wind: Do not underestimate the effect of the wind. A good tailwind can take a great deal of the effort out of cycling; a strong headwind, conversely, will require a much greater effort than still wind conditions. If you are planning to cycle and return along the same leg, try to tackle the upwind direction first and you will then be able to look forward to an easier return trip.

Dress: If you are likely to be riding along busy roads, in towns or at night, make sure you can be seen. Wear a brightly-coloured cycle helmet, shirt, anorak or other outer clothing.

In rain, the decision to put on water proofs or get wet can be a difficult one. For instance, in summer rain, when the ambient temperature is higher, you may be far more comfortable just getting soaked and not bothering with waterproofs. Initially, if you are undecided, always put on the waterproofs. If you do get too hot it is easy enough to cool down, but getting dried off is a longer and more demanding process. Once you have become wet, waterproofs become a far less attractive option as they will tend to hold moisture in, which can be quite uncomfortable.

The biggest danger of all in wet conditions is cold. Your body heat can dissipate very quickly because of the combination of wet skin and the wind movement as you cycle along. You can find yourself shivering and in the early stages of hypothermia far more quickly than if you were standing or walking in the same conditions. Even if the waterproofs feel sticky and sweaty to wear, at least you should be warm. Gloves and some form of head-covering are essential wear in wet conditions to avoid further heat loss.

Hiring

Fortunately, the wide availability of cycle hire centres has created a situation whereby you do not need to own a bicycle to enjoy the routes in this book. Use some basic common sense when hiring and consider the following points.

Charges. It is up to you to decide if the charges are fair or not, but do be sure that you know exactly what you are expected to pay. Some hirers quote by the hour, some by the day and some by the week. It is usually worth shopping around.

Deposits. A reasonable cash deposit is normally required. All hirers will, quite reasonably, insist on some form of identification. A driving licence, a credit card or a passport are usually acceptable, either solely or in combination.

Transporting Your Bicycle by Car

There are several methods and each has pros and cons.

Roof rack clamp fittings. Pro: Security, less possibility of damage to the bicycle. Con: Low bridges, putting the bicycle on and taking it off.

Back rack. Pro: Very easy to use. Cheap to buy. Con: Poor security when the car is unattended. Can knock the bicycles about if you are carrying more than one.

Tow bar rack. Pro: Good security, you can D-lock your bike to your car. Ease of use. Con: You need a towbar.

There are a few pitfalls and rules to be aware of.

- ☐ If you have any fast-fix, clip-on equipment such as pumps, drinking bottles, mudguards, pannier sets or anything else that is not welded or screwed to the bicycle, take it off or it will certainly fall off.
- ☐ If you are carrying your bikes by the roof rack method, beware of car park barriers.
- ☐ A bicycle carried transversely on a rack on the back of a car is generally wider than the car itself. If you are travelling along narrow lanes or through tight town streets, allow for that extra width.
- ☐ If you are transporting your bicycle on a back rack, make certain that your bicycle tyres are well clear of the car's exhaust. The hot exhaust gases can melt the tyre.
- ☐ Make sure that your rear lights and number plates are not obscured. If they are, you may need to invest in a number plate and lighting board (your car will need the external socket which is normally used with towbars).

Railways, Buses and Aeroplanes

Railway travel: The services offered to cyclists by train operators are constantly changing. For the latest information, check before you plan to travel and always expect to book because space is limited. In broad terms, most train operators are helpful and well-disposed towards cyclists but demand can be high. On journeys where changes of train are required, you will normally be expected to be responsible for moving your own bicycle, but this would probably be advisable under any circumstances. Remember:

- ☐ Book before you go. (There may be a £3 fee.)

- ☐ Long-distance trains such as sleeper services and Intercity services will have an overall capacity for forty bicycles.
- ☐ "Sprinters" have space for four bicycles per pair of carriages.
- ☐ If in doubt, keep smiling because conductors have discretion beyond these limits if space allows.

Bus travel: Use buses to get back home or get back to a parked car having secured your bicycle in some safe place for later retrieval. It is an easy job to check local services and timetables and plan a day's cycling on this basis, and it is a fantastic way to use a good tailwind! Facilities offered by bus operators for carrying bicycles by bus tend to be fairly sketchy in terms of both detail and availability. Where facilities are available, the costs are usually very high, although some operators actually offer free passage for bicycles. In all cases enquiry and pre-booking are essential.

Air travel: Most airlines will carry bicycles, either within your luggage allowance or at a small additional charge. Some airlines supply special bags free of charge. On pressurised aircraft, ensure that you deflate the tyres otherwise they may burst at altitude due to the reduction in atmospheric pressure. As with all public transport services, the golden rule is to book and enquire before travelling!

Cycling along Towpaths

Canal and river towing-path cycling is recommended as one of the safest and most satisfying forms of leisure cycling, but there are a few special hazards to watch out for.

Ropes: Some boats are secured to the canal side by mooring ropes. Most of these are sensibly and considerately placed to cause the least possible inconvenience to other canal towpath users. Very occasionally you may encounter a boat tied to a tree with the rope at neck level, or perhaps a rope tightened across the towing-path a few inches off the ground. Keep a good look out.

Mooring spikes: Long, metal mooring spikes can also be a problem. These are often very jagged at the top from repeated hammering, and always hard. The very few that are badly positioned are usually easy to see and avoid, but occasionally the sharp edge of a mooring spike may be hidden by long grass or weeds.

Anglers: Anglers using long pole rods often have them projecting across the towing-path behind their backs. Make sure that they know you are passing and give them plenty of time to gather their gear together. A walker can step over rods, buckets, nets and sandwich boxes, but you will require a clear passage.

Potholes at the water's edge: Where the towpath is breaking up, the first major potholes or landslips seem to occur near the water's edge. When you are passing narrow and poorly maintained sections, keep your speed well down or dismount and push until the going improves.

Other Cyclists: If you are riding in a group, never bunch up too tightly. A tiny problem can become serious if cyclists are riding too close to one another. Keep plenty of distance at all times. If you want to pass a slower cyclist, make your intentions clear and wait for a good opportunity.

Obstructions: No matter how good the overall conditions, there are always places on canal towing-paths where a cyclist must get off and push for a while. This should be considered to be part of the canal towpath cycling ritual. There is no place here for any kind of speed work, whether it be racing, fitness routine or simply speeding. Remember, a large part of the joy of towing-path cycling is in the leisurely and relaxed manner of the progress. If you need to push your bicycle for a while, you should view this as part of the pleasure and not consider it to be a nuisance or an unreasonable delay. Starting with the correct attitude will enhance your pleasure and make it easier for you to appreciate these very special surroundings.

Common Notices and Waymarks

Waymarks and notices appear in many different forms and locations – from signs fixed to the street furniture to bits of painted wood nailed to walls or wired to trees. There are waymarks carved in stone, painted on the tarmac, stencilled onto wood, routed into posts and set in concrete.

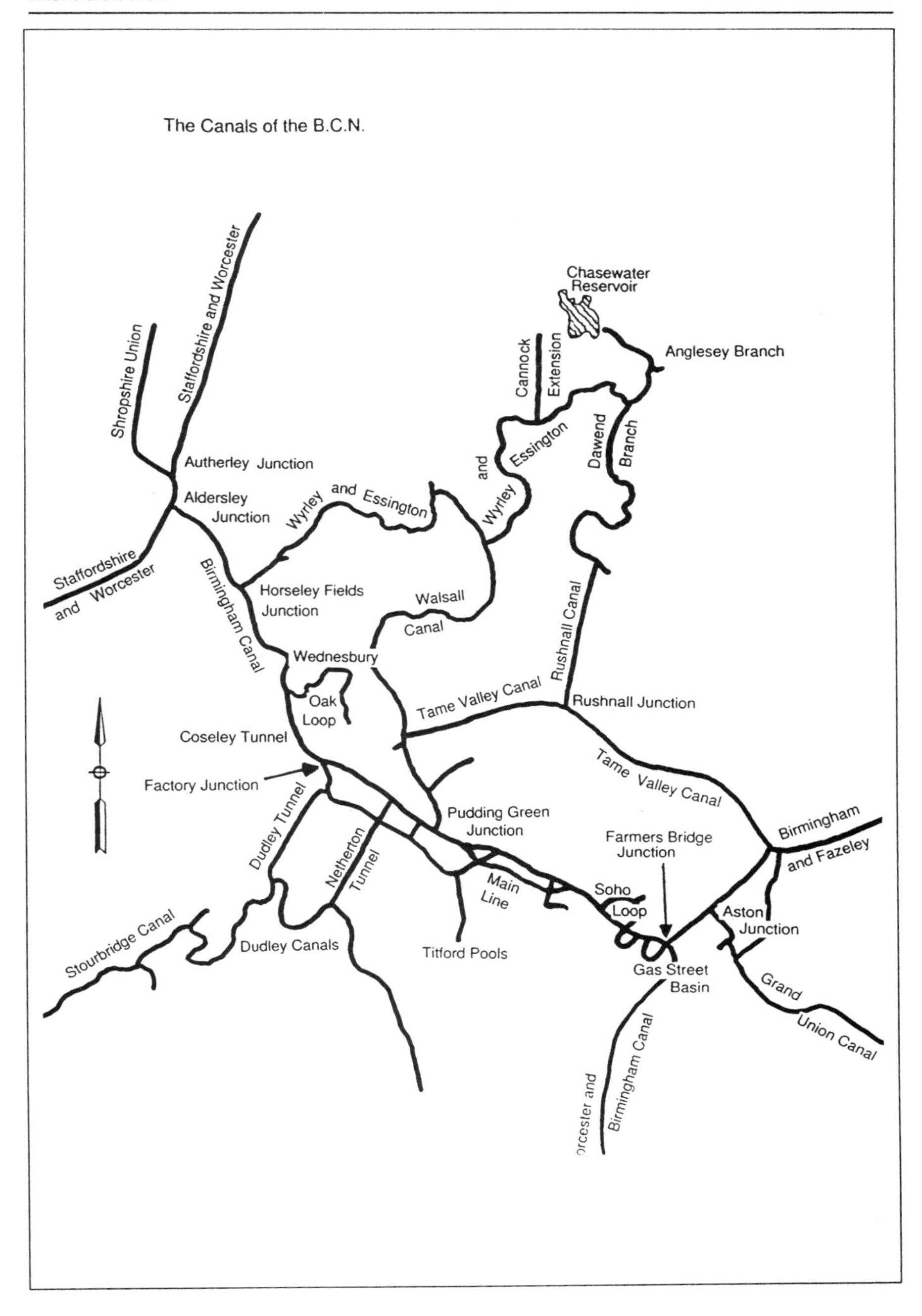
The Canals of the B.C.N.
Staffordshire and Worcester
Shropshire Union
Chasewater Reservoir
Anglesey Branch
Cannock Extension
Dawend Branch
Wyrley and Essington
Autherley Junction
Aldersley Junction
Wyrley and Essington
Staffordshire and Worcester
Birmingham Canal
Horseley Fields Junction
Walsall Canal
Rushnall Canal
Wednesbury
Oak Loop
Tame Valley Canal
Rushnall Junction
Coseley Tunnel
Factory Junction
Tame Valley Canal
Pudding Green Junction
Dudley Tunnel
Netherton Tunnel
Farmers Bridge Junction
Birmingham and Fazeley
Main Line
Soho Loop
Aston Junction
Stourbridge Canal
Dudley Canals
Titford Pools
Gas Street Basin
Grand Union Canal
Birmingham Canal

Unfortunately, waymarking of any particular route will not necessarily be consistent in its format and presentation. The fact that you have seen a run of twelve wooden posts with yellow tops and a routed message saying "Cycle Path" does not mean that the next post is not blue concrete with the message "Bikes". Beware of practical jokers who take delight in turning pointers to send you the wrong way and try to verify the route, especially in or near urban areas where petty vandalism may occur.

Keep a constant lookout for waymarks and try to find a pattern, it will greatly enhance your enjoyment of the ride. If you do come across any vandalism, try to report it to the responsible authority so that they may include the problem in their work schedules.

The National Cycle Network

On the 11th of September 1995, the cycling charity Sustrans (an acronym based on the expression "sustainable transport") were awarded £42 million of lottery funds towards the cost of building Millennium Routes, the first 2500 miles of a national cycle network. The balance required will come from charitable contributions and local authority partners.

The National Cycle Network (NCN) will create a national infrastructure of continuous, high quality, safe and attractive routes reaching all areas of the United Kingdom. Around 2400 miles (3860 km) of route will be available by the year 2000 and this will have grown substantially by the year 2005. The NCN will continue to grow as its popularity encourages further extensions and links – indeed, such is the enthusiasm of around 400 local authorities that the total planned mileage is already well beyond 6000 (9660 km). The NCN will provide several high quality main routes through Birmingham. As with previous transport infra-structures, Birmingham will become a local network hub with routes heading off to all points of the compass. Overall, the network will come within two miles of the homes of 20 million people.

Up-to-date details of the NCN are available from Sustrans, 33 King Street, Bristol, BS1 4DZ.

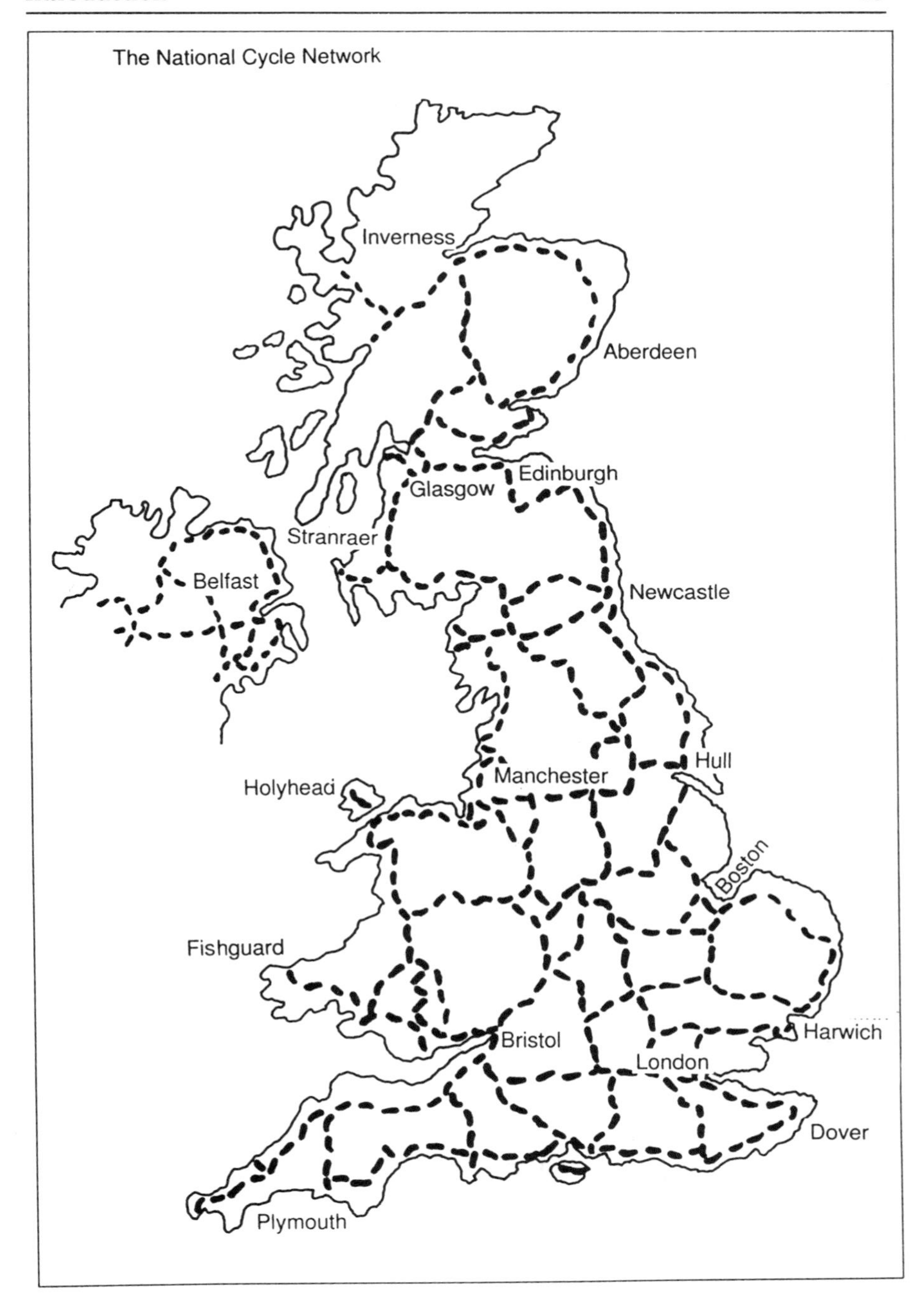
The National Cycle Network
Inverness
Aberdeen
Edinburgh
Glasgow
Stranraer
Belfast
Newcastle
Hull
Manchester
Holyhead
Boston
Fishguard
Harwich
Bristol
London
Dover
Plymouth

Ride 1

The Stafford Greenway

A recreational railway path and canal towpath circular ride via Stafford and the northern outskirts of Wolverhampton.

Maps: Landranger 1:50000 series. Sheet number 127

Distance: 34 miles (55 km)

Waymarked: The Stafford Greenway is well marked. Check bridge numbers and frequent mileposts on the towpath.

Gradients: A flat route except for a few short lock and access gradients.

Surface: Although the Greenway is a recreational path, the surface can be a little bumpy in places. The canal towing-paths are in excellent condition, but, as with all towpath rides, the surface can be muddy when wet.

Future Proposals: None known

Shops and Refreshments: There are plenty of pubs and village shops along the way.

Special Warnings: Watch out for mooring spikes, potholes and ropes.

Permits: British Waterways permit required

This ride, which mainly utilises the magnificent canal towing-paths of the Shropshire Union Canal and the Staffordshire and Worcester Canal, is linked by a most interesting cross-country section along the Stafford Greenway. This delightful recreational railway path is based on the old trackbed of the now long-disused Stafford to Newport Railway. This was built by the Shropshire Union Railway Company, part of the same company which operated the Shropshire Union Canal.

The railway, which was first opened in 1859, formed part of an important trade route into mid-Wales. Its most important function was the carriage of coal and raw materials for the industries of the Black Country and the Potteries. It was closed under the Beeching cuts in the mid 1960s, and was left to nature until an initiative in the late 1980s led to this fine recreational path being opened in the summer of 1991. The surface is not the billiard table smoothness of many ex-railway tracks, but is quiet acceptable for mountain bikes as long as you moderate your pace. There is plenty to see along the way in terms of wildlife and general interest, and the route can easily be extended into the Welsh border areas.

The long canal section is possibly one of the best canal rides in the area. Although for the most part you are in the heart of the main Black Country conurbation, you will find yourself amid nothing but delightful rural scenery and sleepy little villages linked by these lovely stretches of canal. Nearly all of this ride is off-road where the air is fresh and you can safely enjoy the peace and quiet of the countryside, well away from the noise and fuss of traffic and built-up areas.

The Shropshire Union Canal

Access Points

The easiest way to start this ride is by choosing any convenient canal bridge along the route – there are plenty to choose from. You may join the Staffordshire and Worcester canal at Autherley Junction or at any bridge numbered between 67 and 98. The ride follows the Shropshire Union Canal between bridge number 1, by Autherley

Junction, to bridge number 36. The bridge numbers are usually on small metal plaques on the external arch of the structure facing towards canal traffic. Occasionally the plaques are missing but it is never far to the next bridge. A compass is a useful accessory, just in case you become disorientated.

The junction of the Shropshire Union Canal and the Stafford Greenway railway path is situated near the Shropshire Union Canal bridge number 36 at Gnosall Heath.

Another possible starting point is The Sheridan Shopping Centre in Stafford town centre, and for maximum convenience the route notes are taken from here.

The Route

1. Starting at the Sheridan Shopping Centre in the centre of Stafford, turn right into Stafford Street and follow it to the junction at the far end.
2. At the junction at the end of Stafford Street, turn left into Mount Street.
3. Follow Mount Street straight ahead over two mini islands and into Broad Street. At the main traffic island, follow the signposts to Doxey.
4. Before the next mini island, turn left into Castle Street, signposted to Palmbourne Industrial Estate. Follow this road straight ahead, up over the old railway bridge.
5. At the bollards, go straight ahead into the unmade road.
6. Turn right at the mini island and follow this road to the next mini island. Go straight ahead.
7. Go right and immediately left along the tarmac road. You will soon see the Stafford Greenway on your right.
8. Join the Greenway and follow it to Gnosall Heath where it will meet the Shropshire Union Canal by bridge number 36.
9. At bridge number 36 turn right to head south along the towing-path of the canal. The towing-path is on the west of the canal so the water should be on your right as you head south. After about a mile you will come to the 81 metre long Cowley Tunnel

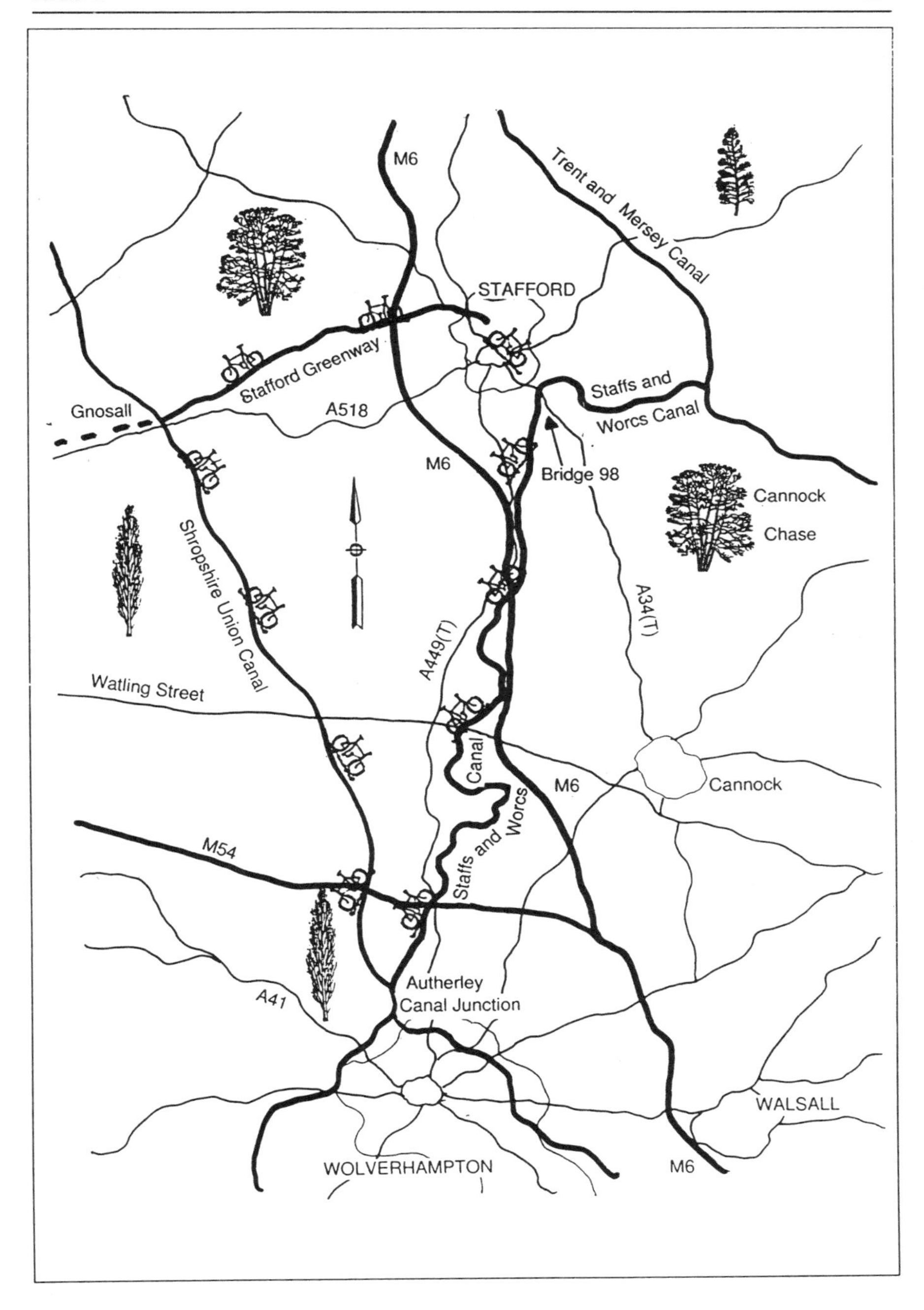
M6
Trent and Mersey Canal
STAFFORD
Stafford Greenway
Gnosall
A518
Staffs and
Worcs Canal
M6
Bridge 98
Cannock
Chase
Shropshire Union Canal
A449(T)
A34(T)
Watling Street
Canal
M6
Cannock
Staffs and Worcs
M54
Autherley
Canal Junction
A41
WALSALL
WOLVERHAMPTON
M6

which is mainly cut through the natural rock. The bridge numbers will be descending (35, 34, 33..).

10. The towpath changes sides at bridge number 26, and then changes back south of Brewood.
11. After about twelve miles along this towing-path, you will come to Autherley Junction. Turn left here by crossing the junction bridge, and then head north along the Staffordshire and Worcester Canal. The water will be on your right and the bridge numbers will be ascending (67, 68, 69..).
12. After just over 16 miles along the Staffordshire and Worcester Canal, go left at bridge number 98 to return to Stafford.

Nearby

The Shropshire Union Canal, The Old Shroppie, as it is affectionately known, is one of the best-preserved and best-loved canals on the whole waterways system. Originally engineered by Thomas Telford, the relatively flat topography surrounding this section of the waterway allowed him to cut bold long straights, utilising low embankments and shallow cuttings. Although the overall purpose of the canal was to transport goods between The Black Country and The Manchester Ship Canal, this southern section enjoyed an excellent local trade, benefiting from its proximity and links with the Welsh border canal system which used to head west from Norbury Junction.

This section passes through some glorious countryside. The towing-path is of consistent good quality and virtually uninterrupted. Features include the 81 metre long Cowley Tunnel and the long Grub Street Cutting which is often used in photographs to typify the character of this canal sector.

Ride 2

Mountain Bike Trail in Cannock Chase

A waymarked mountain bike trail in the wilds of Cannock Chase. It mainly follows ancient bridleways.

Maps: Landranger 1:50000 series. Sheet numbers 127 and 128, or to get the whole route on one sheet try O.S. Explorer, series 6 (Cannock and Chasewater)

Distance: 9 miles (14.5 km)

Waymarked: Green posts with white bicycle symbols routed into the surface and highlighted

Gradients: One or two ups and downs although nearly all on contour tracks suitable for Land-Rovers and trucks

Surface: Mainly forest vehicle tracks. Can be muddy and slippery, especially when wet.

Future Proposals: Further links are planned to join Forest Enterprise routes planned from the Forestry Visitor Centre.

Shops and Refreshments: Mainly limited to the Marquis Drive Visitor Centre

Special Warnings: Check for any special warnings at the Marquis Drive visitor centre and always obey warning signs in the forest.

Permits: N/A

The origins of Cannock Chase date back to the reign of William the Conqueror. A vast area, of which the modern Cannock Chase was just a part, was set aside as a hunting ground known as King's Forest of Cannock. Over the years the original hunting ground has reduced in size, mainly to make way for the growth of the northern conurbation of Birmingham and the Black Country towns such as Wolverhampton and Walsall. Ownership was passed from the crown to the church and then onto the Paget family who developed the vast iron deposits in the area. Later the forest paid a massive toll to industry, which included losing nearly all of its oak woodlands to satisfy the vast demand for charcoal.

The accelerating demand for coal from about 1800 onwards saw the area become a massive coalfield, dotted with numerous small mining settlements and heavily reliant on the whims of the heavy industries of the Black Country. Canals and railways improved the communications of the area. In the early 20th century, large parts of the forest were occupied by the military for training camps, German POW camps and an army hospital.

Arguably, the modern history of Cannock Chase begins in 1957 when the 3rd Earl of Lichfield gifted over 800 hectares (2000 acres) to the county council. In 1958 the area which we now know as Cannock Chase Country Park was identified as an area of outstanding natural beauty (AONB) and today offers a superb recreational retreat, an ideal spot for physical and mental relaxation and for lovers of wildlife. There are great tracts of open heath, stream side wetlands which are ideal for picnics, woodland, modern forest and many sites of special scientific and archaeological interest. Information about all this can be found at the superb Marquis Drive visitor centre.

Waymarks across Cannock Chase

This ride, which was first waymarked in the summer of 1996, starts at the visitor centre and follows waymarks through the forest and plantations. It is designed for mountain bikes and it is quite suitable for families and beginners as well as experts. There are various short cuts along the way and numerous quiet resting spots. The main part of the ride is along forest Land Rover tracks which can be churned up in very wet conditions, but can offer a delightful surface in the dry.

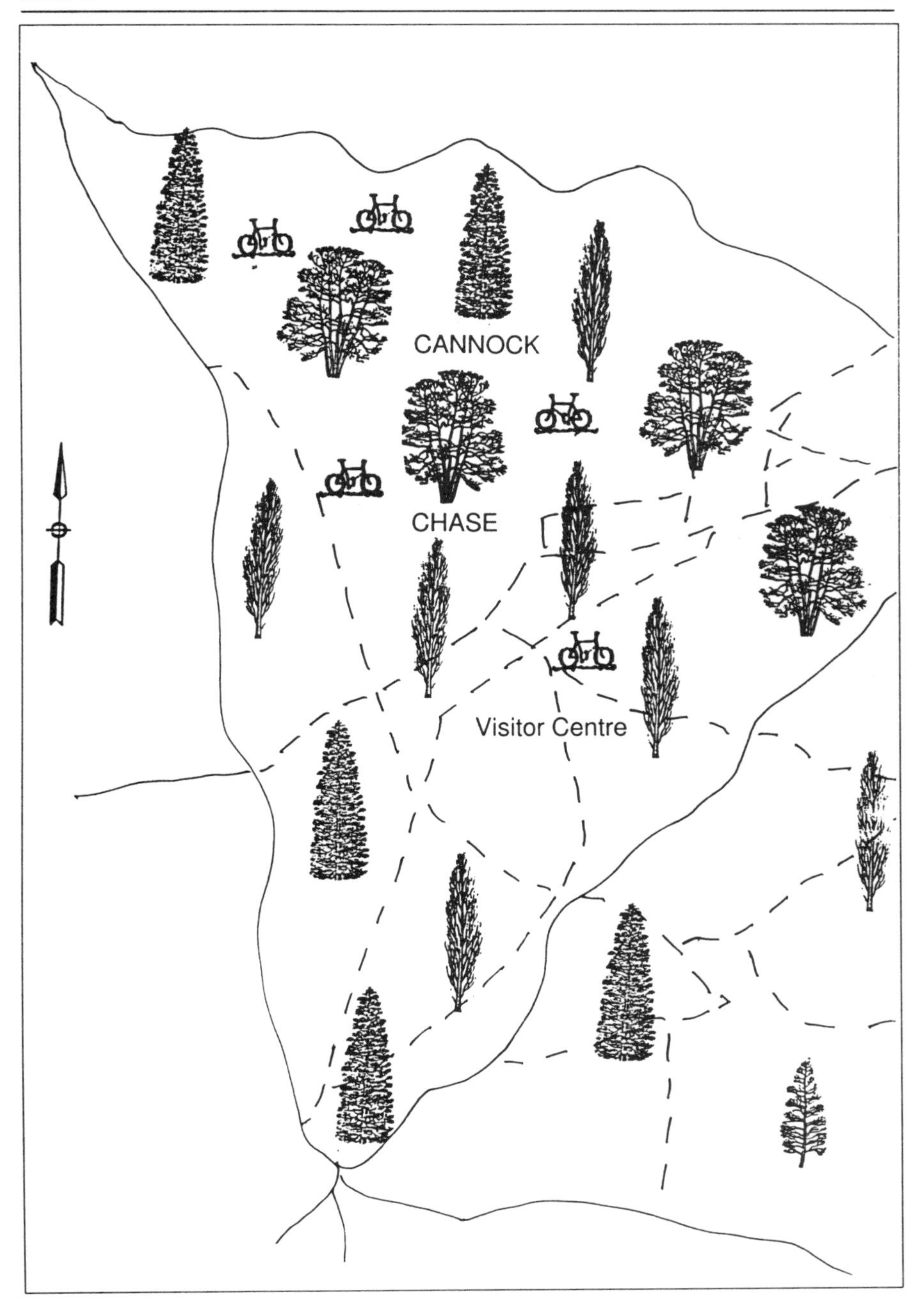
CANNOCK
CHASE
Visitor Centre

Access Points

Start the ride from the Marquis Drive visitor centre. The first waymarks can easily be seen from the car park. The visitor centre is situated about a mile and a half north of Hednesford and is clearly signposted off the Brindley Valley Road. There is another possible starting point and a car park at Seven Springs, just south of Little Haywood village, by Weetman's Bridge just off the A513. If you are planning a shorter ride than the whole nine mile circuit (perhaps with children), the Seven Springs car park may be a better choice.

The Route

1. The start of the main waymarked route is easily found from the car park at Marquis Drive visitor centre. After leaving the car park area heading in a roughly northerly direction, you are soon in the forest. The main backbone of the route follows the stream which runs along Sherbrook Valley to Stepping Stones and then onto Seven Springs, returning through Abraham's Valley. There is an easy cutback return route after the first few miles
2. A shorter route, perhaps suitable for children, can easily be devised by starting at the northern extremity of the ride at the car park at Seven Springs, using well-established Land Rover tracks and bridleways. From Seven Springs, follow the waymarks south west along Abraham's Valley and then, as the main trail turns south, take the alternative track north west to join the main waymarked route just south of Stepping Stones.
3. As a general rule, if the track is wide enough for a Land Rover and as long as there are no signs prohibiting cycling, you are free to roam in the forest. If the track is narrow or grassy it will not normally be suitable for cycling.

Nearby

The Valley Heritage Centre and Museum is on the outskirts of Hednesford. It is a fascinating place and well worth a visit. It tells the story of the area and particularly of Cannock Chase, tracing its fascinating history, its natural development and its diverse industrial connections.

Ride 3

Chasewater Reservoir to Lichfield Cathedral

A delightful rural ride through quiet villages and along little country lanes.

Maps: Landranger 1:50000 series. Sheet numbers 128 and 139

Distance: 24 miles (38.5 km)

Waymarked: No

Gradients: No major climbs but a few short ones

Surface: Mainly tarmac country lanes, some urban roads. A short section of reasonably good and smooth canal towing-path

Future Proposals: N/A

Shops and Refreshments: Plenty of villages, pubs and shops along the route

Special Warnings: N/A

Permits: N/A

This ride, possibly more than most in this guide, demonstrates just how beautiful and quiet English country lanes can be, even when they are in close proximity to a busy trunk road system. We all realise that most major routes head for major centres and thus radiate from these centres like spokes from the hub of a wheel. In the initial stage of planning this route there did not appear to be an obvious way around this particular very busy road pattern. It seemed that the area would prove fairly uninviting, possibly even unsuitable for leisure cycling. Initial impressions could hardly have been more wrong; by crossing and re-crossing these radial roads at roughly right angles there emerges a superb cycle route which, by any standards, is exceptionally safe and useable.

In the final outcome this route is only broadly affected by the trunk roads, in the sense that they are a constant surprise and reminder of your relatively close proximity to the heart of the Black Country. If you are familiar with the main roads around this area, you will be amazed at the contrast. If you are an outsider, make a point of trying this route and you will find a bit of England that is largely unspoilt by the march of progress.

Just outside Lichfield are the old Roman remains of Letocetum, and it is well worth the effort to divert to the site. You will find this an enjoyable, informative and thought-provoking visit.

Access Points

Chacewater reservoir is situated to the north of the A5(T), just about a mile north of Brownhills. There is plenty of car parking within the reservoir complex. A good alternative start and finish point is Lichfield Cathedral. There are good train services here, as well as car parking and all the facilities you would expect in a cathedral city.

The Route

1. From the southern end of Chacewater Reservoir, head east out of the complex. Turn left out of the main gate, by the Warden's office.
2. After a short distance you will cross a small bridge over an outflow from the reservoir. Just beyond this bridge, a track forks to the right and descends to the canal. Follow the track around the head of the canal terminus and then follow the towing-path on the northern side of the canal, heading east.
3. At the first bridge, leave the towpath and turn left along Wharf Lane to head north.
4. At the crossroads at the end of Wharf Lane (the junction with the B5011, Hanney Hay Road), turn right and then, after a short distance, go straight ahead at the crossroads into a rural lane.
5. You are now heading roughly south. Shortly after crossing under the railway you will arrive at a crossroads junction with the A5(T). Cross straight over with care, and continue along the lane opposite.
6. After a very short distance, you will arrive at another crossroads junction with the B4155. Go straight ahead into Barracks Lane.

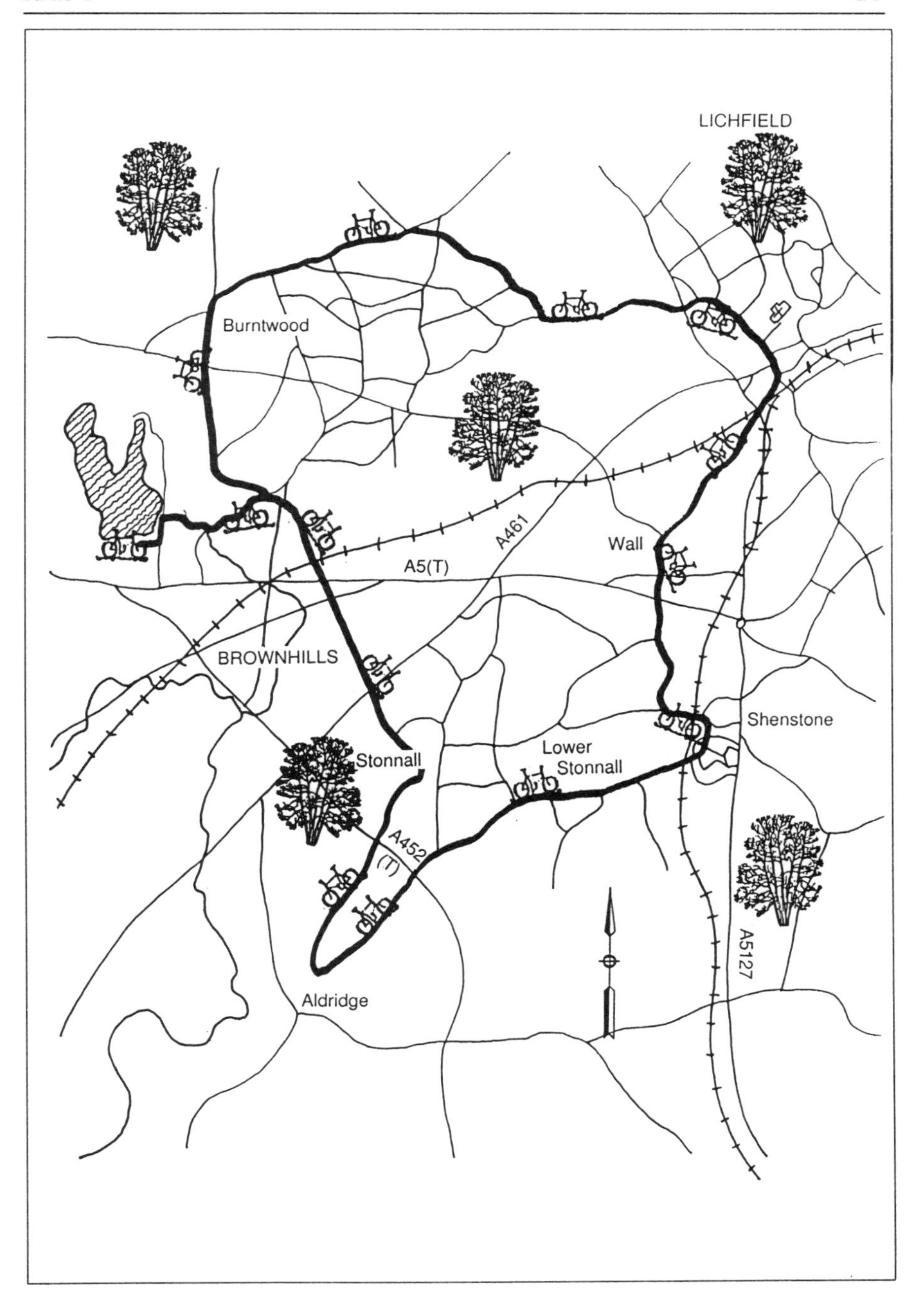
LICHFIELD
Burntwood
A461
Wall
A5(T)
BROWNHILLS
Shenstone
Lower
Stonnall
Stonnall
A452
(T)
A5127
Aldridge

7. Continue for almost a mile until you arrive at a crossroads junction with the A461 dual carriageway trunk road. Crossing with care, go straight on into Cartersfield Lane.
8. In just over half a mile you will arrive in the village of Stonnall and come to a T-junction. Turn right here.
9. After about another half a mile you will arrive at a crossroads junction with the A452(T). Go straight on here into Lazy Hill, Stonnall.
10. You will soon arrive in the built-up area known as Lazy Hill at a crossroads junction surrounded by shops and a pub. Go left here.
11. In a short distance go left again, following the signpost to Druid's Heath Golf Club. Follow this road away from the built-up area.
12. At the crossroads junction with the A52(T), go straight ahead into Gravelly Lane and follow the road signposted to Shenstone.
13. On the edge of Shenstone village, turn left and follow the road across the railway.
14. At the crossroads at the end of Footherley Road, turn left into New Road.
15. At the T-junction at the end of New Road, turn left (signposted to Stonnall and Aldridge) and follow the main road a short distance to cross the railway.
16. Shortly after crossing the railway, turn right into Ashcroft Lane, signposted to Wall and Chesterfield.
17. Now heading north, this road goes under the A5(T) before passing through the old village of Wall. Follow the road signposted to Lichfield.
18. Arriving in Lichfield, go left along the Birmingham Road and follow the signposts to the city centre.
19. After exploring the city centre and the Cathedral, with your back to the main door of the cathedral, facing south-west, head back to the main road and turn right to head west.
20. Just after the supermarket mini-roundabout, on the edge of Lichfield, go left into Abnall's Lane.

21. After a short distance, you will come to the main A51. Cross over this road to continue along Abnall's Lane which is opposite and slightly to the right, signposted to Chorley.
22. A short way along this lane, go right, signposted to Chorley. Follow the road up to Chorley Village.
23. At the crossroads by The Malt Shovel public house, turn left, signposted to Boney Hay and Chase Terrace.
24. Follow this road through the outskirts of Burntwood and eventually you will come to a T-junction. Go left onto the B5011, signposted to Chase Terrace.
25. Follow this long, straight road through the built-up area and eventually, after crossing over traffic lights, you will come to a sharp left-hand bend. Follow this bend around and continue down the hill.
26. At the bottom of the hill, turn right into Wharf Lane and retrace your route back to Chacewater Reservoir via the canal towpath.

Nearby

The 13th century Lichfield Cathedral with its three famous spires is particularly striking. It enjoys an idyllic cloistered setting, surrounded by superbly preserved 14th to 16th century houses and an impressive 17th century Bishop's Palace.

Lichfield Cathedral

Around the west front there are over 100 statues.

The history of the old Roman settlement at Wall, known as Letocetum Roman Town, is explained in the exhibits of Wall Museum. The most complete Roman bath house to date was found on this site, which is based on the crossroads of two major routes, Ryknild Street and Watling Street.

Ride 4

Cycling in Sutton Park

The grand beauty of Sutton Park via safe tarmac roads and trails.

Maps: Landranger 1:50000 series. Sheet number 139

Distance: A typical ride approx. 5 miles (8 km)

Waymarked: Follow the hard roads and obey any no cycling signs.

Gradients: Nothing to worry about, just a few gentle slopes.

Surface: Made up tarmac and gravelled park roads.

Future Proposals: N/A

Shops and Refreshments: There are café facilities in the park, at the visitor centre and by the gates in the summer.

Special Warnings: Pedestrians

Permits: N/A

Sutton Park (1000 hectares, 2400 acres) has its origins as a medieval deer park with early references dating back to the 12th century. In later centuries it provided wood for the people of Sutton and grazing meadows for their animals. During the 17th and 18th centuries, the park became lightly industrialised with water mills powering the early crude machines. Since the 19th century the park has provided a mainly recreational area, but has also been host to troops and mass ordnance during the two world wars. Within the park are streams, lakes, woods and open spaces, all preserved in their natural states.

The park was originally given to the town of Sutton in 1558. It was secured by John Veysey, Bishop of Exeter, who died in 1554, apparently at the amazing old age of 102. His ideal was to provide useful common land for the local population, and in the modern sense his idea is still as successful today as it was in 1555.

Sutton Park is an ideal venue for safe off-road cycling, general leisure cycling and basic fitness cycling. With its wealth of hard-surfaced, traffic-free roadways, it is a great place to enjoy an hour or so in the saddle. Birmingham City Council promote Sutton Park as

'A Park for All The People' and it is difficult to word a better short description. This sort of cycling venue is ideal for children to get used to the prospect of venturing out on their bikes and, of course, a great place to teach young children the basic skills of riding on two wheels (much easier on a very slight downhill incline).

Safe cycling in Sutton Park

Within the boundary of the park you will find vast open spaces; sheltered, wooded plantations and several attractive pools. Wildlife abounds and there are endless sheltered resting spots.

Access Points

As well as the main Town Gate, there are entrance gates to the park all around its perimeter. There is no fixed itinerary for this ride, simply get on your bike from any gate and enjoy the traffic-free cycling available.

A452(T)
Roman Road
Memorial
Visitor
Centre
SUTTON
COLDFIELD
A4041
Banner's
Gate
Golf
A453

The Route

Birmingham City Council Leisure and Community Services department publish a useful leaflet entitled "Cycling in Sutton Park". The leaflet gives some useful safety tips and there is a clear map which shows you where you may and may not cycle, and where you are in relation to the surrounding road system. A copy of this leaflet is available from the visitor centre which is situated just behind Wyndley Leisure Centre, just inside the Town Gate main park entrance.

In the absence of the leaflet, simply stick to the main park roads and keep off the golf course and the nature conservation areas. Obey any signs and you will not go far wrong.

Nearby

The town of Sutton Coldfield was independent of Birmingham until 1974 when it was incorporated as part of the city. It still retains a very independent atmosphere and has a superb shopping centre as well as well-respected schools and a first class leisure and youth centre.

The remains of the old Roman road, Icknield Street, can be seen by the western boundary of the park. The immediate northern continuation of this Roman road forms one of the finest residential areas of Sutton Coldfield.

Ride 5

Along The Birmingham and Fazeley canal

A linear route from Spaghetti Junction to Tamworth via the superb towing-path of the Birmingham and Fazeley Canal.

Maps: Landranger 1:50000 series. Sheets number 139 and 140

Distance: Return ride twenty four miles (38.5 km)

Waymarked: Plenty of bridge numbers and mileposts.

Gradients: None.

Surface: Canal towpath, generally suitable for mountain bikes or wide-tyred tourers. Easy cycling conditions with the occasional inevitable slippery and narrow patch. Very treacherous underfoot in Curdworth Tunnel.

Future Proposals: British Waterways has a policy of constant maintenance and improvement.

Shops and Refreshments: Plenty of stopping off places reached from the numerous bridges.

Special Warnings: Some sections of this towing-path can be particularly slippery when wet. Watch out for mooring spikes and ropes. Do not try to cycle through the tunnel – get off and push.

Permits: British Waterways permit required.

The Birmingham and Fazeley Canal forms an essential link between the Birmingham Canal Navigations (BCN) and Coventry Canal to the east. The Coventry canal then connects with the Oxford Canal to the south, and the Trent and Mersey Canal to the north. The Birmingham and Fazeley received considerable opposition before it was authorised by Parliament in 1784. Most of the criticism came from The Birmingham Canal Company which was certain to lose substantial traffic to this new venture. When the building of The Birmingham and Fazeley Canal became a certainty, however, the rift between the two companies became a merger known initially as The Birmingham and Birmingham and Fazeley Canal Company (BBFCC). Not long after the merger this newly formed company dropped its breathless title and came to be known simply as The

Birmingham Canal Company. In this form it went on to be one the most financially successful canal companies of the whole waterways era.

The Birmingham and Fazeley Canal

The conception of the Birmingham and Fazeley Canal was the catalyst that brought about the completion of the Coventry Canal and the final extension of the Oxford Canal. John Smeaton was the engineer employed in this construction. He completed his work in 1789, only five years after the original parliamentary authorisation. Far from being worried about too little business, as some early objectors had suggested, the Birmingham and Fazeley Canal's problem was congestion, especially on the Farmer's Bridge and Aston Lock flights into Birmingham. This led to the building of The Tame Valley Canal and The Birmingham and Warwick Junction Canal, both of which were opened in 1844 as relief lines to the Birmingham and Fazeley Canal.

The towing-path provides an excellent cycling surface for mountain bikes. The surroundings are interesting and varied, but this towpath, like many, can be slippery and potentially treacherous in very wet conditions. There are, however, plenty of pubs along the way and no shortage of bridges from which you can normally leave the canal towing-path.

Access Points

Two suggested access points are Salford Junction under Spaghetti Junction or Fazeley Junction near Tamworth, where the Coventry Canal and The Birmingham and Fazeley Canal meet (see Ride 18). There are numerous bridges along the route and it is easy to join from most of them. Kingsbury Water Park (see Ride 6) is close to the canal.

There are excellent rail links to Gravelly Hill and to Tamworth. Refer to British Rail for up-to-date information. Long-distance rail links can be made directly from Birmingham.

The Route

1. Begin at Salford Junction under the Spaghetti road and railway interchange with your back to the main BCN and central Birmingham. Turn right towards Fazeley Junction along the main line canal. (Do not take the second right along the Warwick Junction Canal towards Bordesley Junction.)
2. You will soon pass under an unusual "roofed" section of canal under a building just before Erdington Hall bridge.
3. After about three miles you will pass the first of the three descending Minworth locks.
4. After another half a mile you will pass the second descending Minworth lock.
5. Just after Forge Lane Bridge, pass under the railway, pass the third descending Minworth lock and then pass under the A38(T).
6. About five and half miles from Salford Junction, you will need to dismount for the 57 metre long Curdworth Tunnel. Take care because the path is treacherous underfoot.
7. Beyond the tunnel you will begin to pass the eleven descending locks of the Curdworth flight and pass under the A446(T).

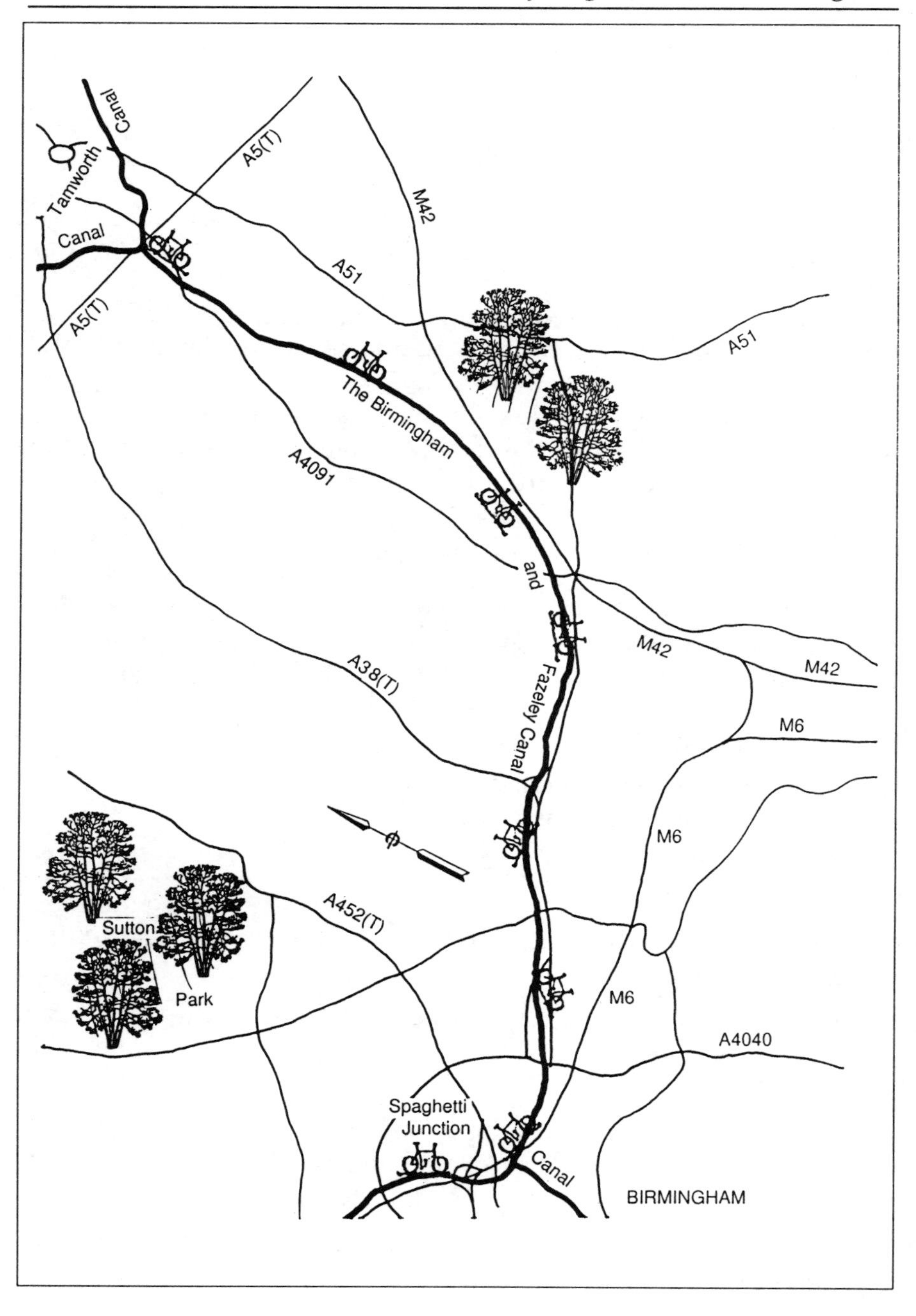
Tamworth
Canal
Canal
A5(T)
A5(T)
M42
A51
A51
The Birmingham
and
Fazeley Canal
A4091
A38(T)
M42
M42
M6
M6
M6
A452(T)
Sutton
Park
A4040
Spaghetti
Junction
Canal
BIRMINGHAM

8. After passing eight further locks, pass under Bodymoor Heath Bridge.
9. Pass the last two of the eleven descending locks of the Curdworth flight and about a mile and a half later, after passing Drayton Manor Park and Zoo, you will arrive at Fazeley Junction. Go right at Watling Street Bridge (A5) for Fazeley village and public houses.

Nearby

The cycling along the first (Spaghetti Junction) section of the canal is excellent and the surroundings can offer hours of interest to the industrial archaeologist or amateur historian. There are numerous wharves, both old and new, and the very special experience of cycling under the Gravelly Hill Interchange (Spaghetti Junction). Here road, rail and canal exist together in an immensely complex web of steel, water and concrete. It is a common sight to see a peaceful angler enjoying the relaxation of his sport while the world goes mad all around his ears. Beyond Gravelly Hill, in any direction, the world gradually becomes a more peaceful place. The countryside along this stretch is pleasant but fairly bland, and eventually the towing-path arrives unceremoniously at Fazeley Junction.

Ride 6

Kingsbury Water Park

A very safe, off-road family cycling facility by the waterside.

Maps: Landranger 1:50000 series. Sheet number 139

Distance: Over three miles (5 km)

Waymarked: Waymarked routes throughout the 240 hectare (600 acre) water park

Gradients: Very easy

Surface: Consolidated pathways and trails.

Future Proposals: N/A

Linking Rides: There is direct access from the Birmingham and Fazeley Canal towing-path.

Shops and Refreshments: Kingsbury Water Park Visitor Centre café

Special Warnings: Take heed of warnings and safety information in the visitor centre.

Permits: N/A

Kingsbury Water Park is a great example of industrial reclamation based on man-made lakes and pools, formerly scars created by 50 or more years of gravel extraction. In the early 1970s work began to reclaim the landscape and there are now some 240 hectares (600 acres) of park containing 30 lakes and pools. Features include woodland walks, games and picnic areas, a campsite, an adventure playground, a shop and visitor centre, a café and a rare breeds farm. Other activities include cycling, fishing, canoeing, powerboating, wind-surfing, sailing, orienteering and horse riding

The waterside bridleways and trails are ideal for playing about on bikes, especially for youngsters and novice cyclists who wish to gain confidence before venturing out onto public roads. On a sunny summer's day this is a lovely spot. Information about the available paths and trails can be obtained from the visitor centre.

Kingsbury Water Park Visitor Centre

Access Points

To find Kingsbury Water Park from the A4091 or the A4097, follow Bodymoor Heath Lane. There is a charge for car parking, but cycles may enter for free. To get to the water park by bicycle from Birmingham or Tamworth, use the towing-path of the Birmingham and Fazeley Canal.

The Route

Although there are waymarks and suggestions from the visitor centre, this is a great place to simply go as you please. It is superbly suitable for children to explore for the sake of the sheer pleasure of riding their bikes in safety – free from traffic, enclosed, miles of trail and endless places to sit and enjoy a picnic. If you are new to cycling or simply want a pleasurable bike ride with the family, this is a great venue.

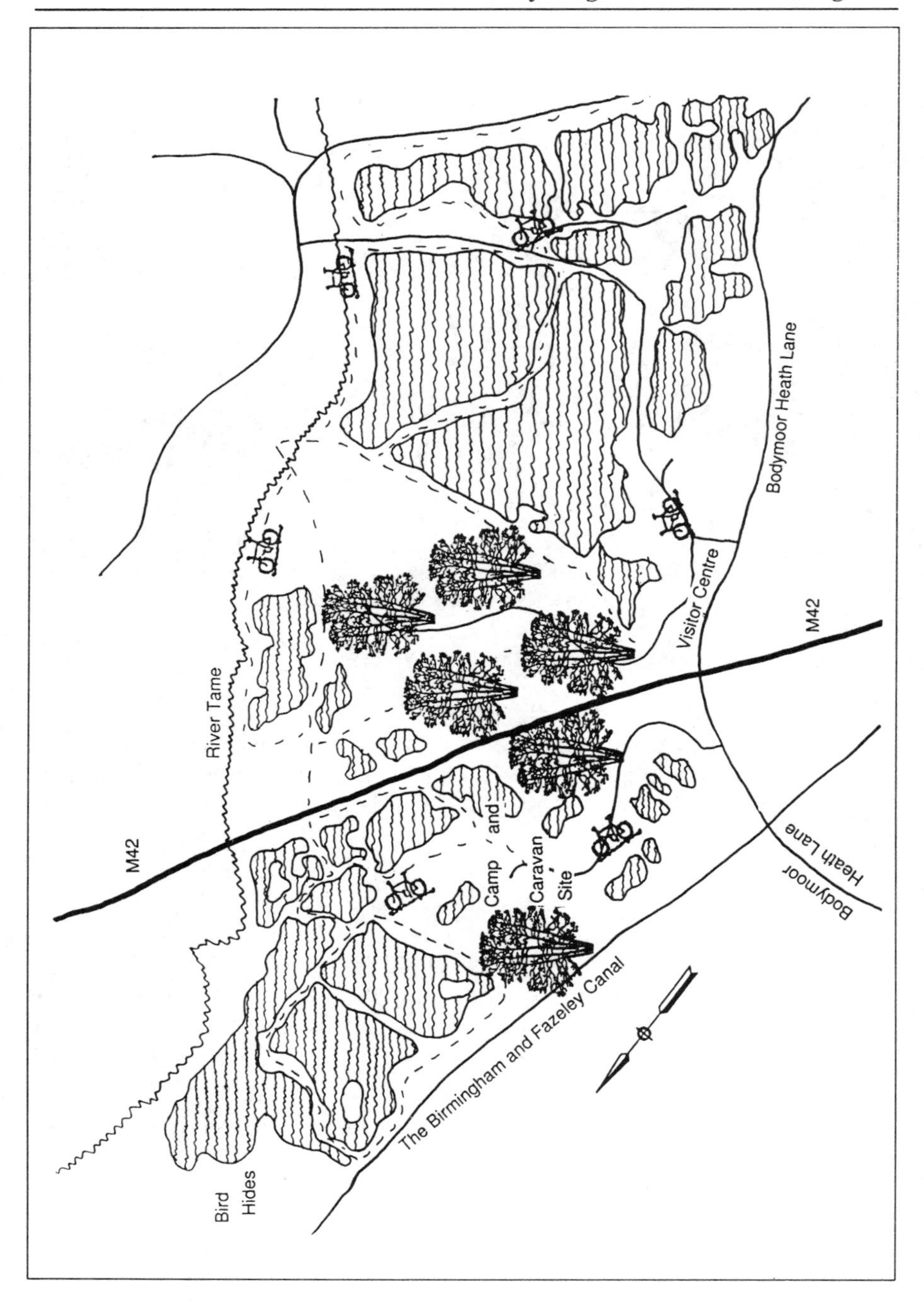
Bodymoor Heath Lane
Visitor Centre
M42
River Tame
M42
Camp and Caravan Site
Bodymoor Heath Lane
The Birmingham and Fazeley Canal
Bird Hides

Nearby

Drayton Manor Park and Zoo is situated south of Tamworth, off the A409 and along the eastern bank of the Birmingham and Fazeley Canal. Drayton Manor was originally the house of Sir Robert Peel but has now become a popular tourist attraction. Within its 6 hectares (15 acres) of wood and parkland are monkeys, exotic birds, lions, pumas, llamas, bears and sea-lions.

Ride 7

The Birmingham and Black Country Cycleway

An industrial and semi-rural discovery trail based on the Birmingham and Black Country off-road, towpath cycleway. Passing close to the Black Country Museum.

Maps: Landranger 1:50000 series. Sheet number 139

Distance: 15 miles (24 km)

Waymarked: A straightforward linear route with a combination of clear signs, mileposts, lock numbers and bridge numbers.

Gradients: A flat towing-path route

Surface: A first class cycling surface. Beware of extremely bumpy brick setts under bridge holes which can come as a shock after long stretches of flat, hard surface.

Future Proposals: British Waterways is always looking at new ways of improving its facilities.

Shops and Refreshments: Take any bridge exit along the route and you will not be very far from a shop or a pub. There are also a few canal side shops and pubs.

Special Warnings: Beware of mooring spikes and ropes. A few narrow and potentially slippery sections, but these are normally quite short. Push through the tunnel and do not rely on the safety rail.

Permits: British Waterways permit required.

The Birmingham and Black Country off-road cycleway follows the towing-paths of the main line canals from the centre of Birmingham to Wolverhampton. It has been designated a cycleway and recreational route since the early 1990s, but its previous history and its relevance to Birmingham is the real fascination.

When the Birmingham Canal Navigations became congested with too much traffic (just like our modern motorway system), the powers that existed at the time decided to build a bypass to ease the bottleneck. Advances in the confidence and technology of the canal engineers meant that the engineer, Thomas Telford, took a very different approach to the original engineer, James Brindley. Telford drove his navigation in a straight line through hills and over valleys in a series of cuttings and embankments (cut and fill technique) instead of using the earlier style of building which followed existing contours in a series of bends and gentle loops.

The resultant old and new canals between Gas Street Basin and Factory Junction are, therefore, a great contrast of style. The old Wolverhampton level gently curves and curls its way along, offering a new surprise around every corner. Some of this old line now remains in enormous waterway lay-bys known as Oozells Loop, Soho Loop and Icknield Street Loop. The new Birmingham level, on the other hand, dispenses with curves and thrusts its way boldly through the city in long straight lines. Although this cycle route follows the designated cycleway, there is nothing to stop you exploring these loops and branches. But do take care as the BCN system is vast and without a proper map you could easily find yourself many miles off your intended course.

This ride will particularly show you the contrast between Brindley's old style and Telford's new style of canal building and let you see the interface between the two systems. You will be able to see how industries have come and gone along the waterway and how modern development is making the very best use of this precious facility. You are bound to draw parallels with our modern road system. The older roads seen by the way tend to curve and twist to hold onto contours, where modern roads tend to sweep along in gracious long straights and curves, showing little or no regard for local landscape and contour characteristics.

Access Points

Gas Street Basin/Farmer's Bridge Junction, Birmingham. There is good all day car parking here and the rail links could hardly be better.

The Route

1. From Gas Street Basin, on the Worcester and Birmingham Canal, with the water on your right, go north for the short distance to Farmer's Bridge Junction.
2. Cross the Birmingham and Fazeley Canal at Farmer's Bridge Junction and turn left along the towpath of the Birmingham Level Main Line Canal, signposted to Wolverhampton.

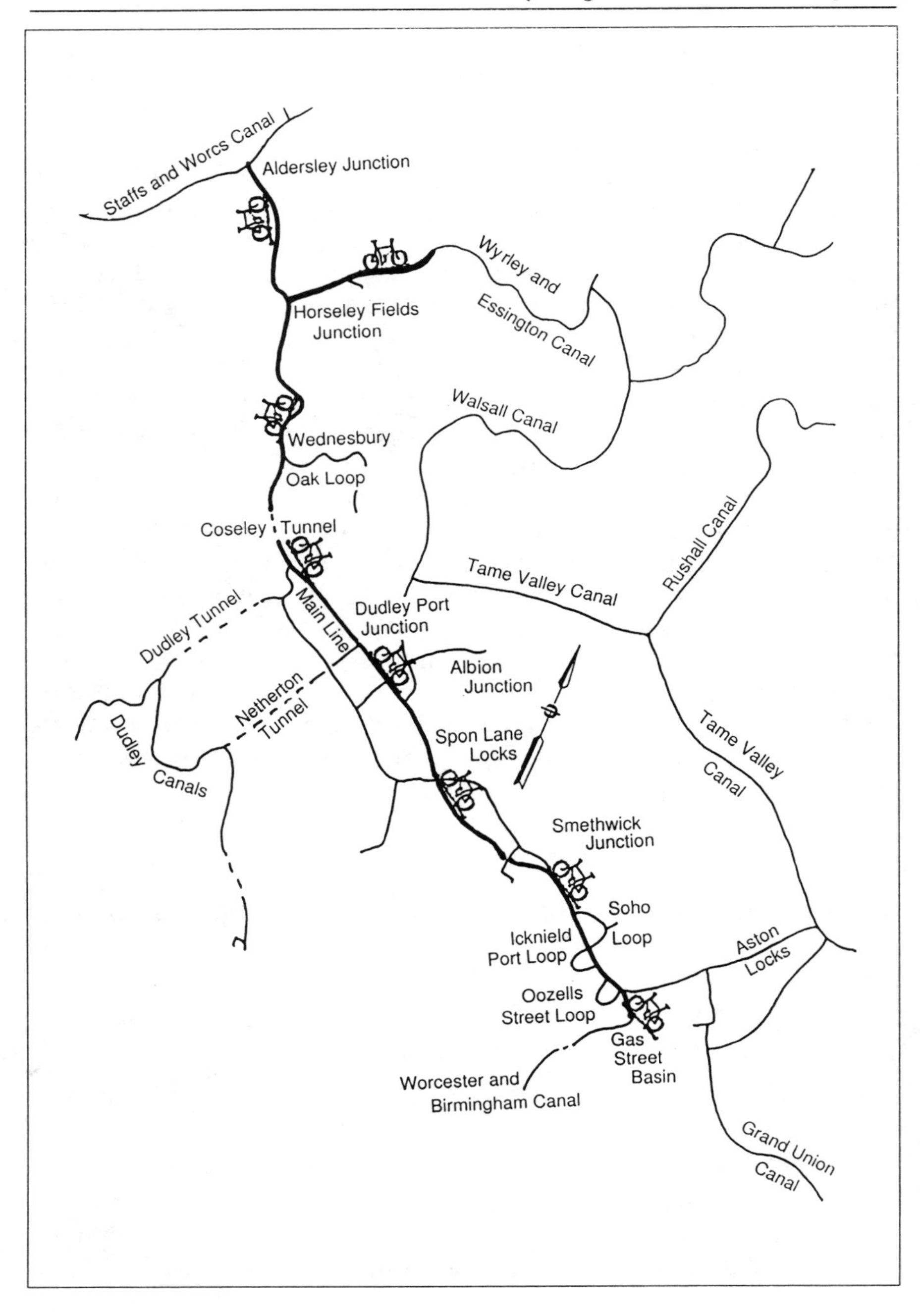

Staffs and Worcs Canal
Aldersley Junction
Wyrley and Essington Canal
Horseley Fields Junction
Walsall Canal
Wednesbury Oak Loop
Coseley Tunnel
Rushall Canal
Tame Valley Canal
Dudley Tunnel
Main Line
Dudley Port Junction
Albion Junction
Netherton Tunnel
Dudley Canals
Spon Lane Locks
Tame Valley Canal
Smethwick Junction
Soho Loop
Icknield Port Loop
Aston Locks
Oozells Street Loop
Gas Street Basin
Worcester and Birmingham Canal
Grand Union Canal

3. After passing the Oozells Street Loop and the Icknield Port Loop, both on the opposite side of the canal, you will come to the junction bridge over the entrance to the Soho Loop. Either turn right into the loop, which is part of the old main line system (if you take this option you will re-emerge approximately 1½ miles later onto the main line) or carry on straight ahead along the main line by crossing the bridge over the exit junction of the Soho Loop.
4. About three miles from Farmer's Bridge, just before Smethwick Junction of the new main line and the old main line, cross the water and pass the junction on the Birmingham Level Canal by keeping left.
5. After about another half mile, pass through Galton Tunnel.
6. Half a mile beyond the tunnel you will pass under the old main line as it crosses overhead on Stewart Aqueduct. You may access the old main line via a twisty path on your right or at Bromford Junction a little further along if you wish explore.
7. Another half mile will bring you to the old main line as it slips in to join the new main line at Bromford Junction by descending a three lock flight from your right. If you want to explore the old main line, this is a good point to cross over.
8. After about another three quarters of a mile you will see Pudding Green Junction on your right. Continue straight ahead towards Wolverhampton.
9. You are now in a fairly open and exposed section with the main line railway on your right. The next two junctions on your left are Albion Junction and Dudley Port Junction. Continue straight on along the main line.
10. After passing Factory Junction on your left, you will come to Coseley Tunnel. Get off and push through the tunnel, keeping the water on your left. Beware of the weak railings.
11. About half a mile from the northern portal of Coseley Tunnel, you will come to the Wednesbury Oak Loop at Deepfields Junction. Carry straight ahead along the main line. You are now about ten miles from Farmer's Bridge Junction.

12. After about another two miles you will come to Horseley Fields Junction (the Wyrley and Essington Canal). From here you can reach Wolverhampton along the cycleway or, alternatively, see 14.
13. Continue past Horseley Fields Junction to Aldersley Junction with the Staffordshire and Worcestershire Canal. You will pass the famous Wolverhampton Lock flight which lifts the canal into the BCN. After exploring, retrace your route back to Gas Street Basin.

Nearby

Whilst riding along this route you will have a chance to see first-hand the amazing contrast between the old and the new, the dereliction and the rejuvenation. One of the least desirable areas is Spon Lane Junction where a large metal reprocessing plant and a motorway on vast concrete stilts hammer home the presence of the twentieth century at work. In contrast, one of the most desirable areas within this circuit is along the old main line where the canal has been utilised as a central feature in housing redevelopment schemes to great effect. Here is displayed the twentieth century at home and its appreciation of the old waterway as a recreational asset.

The old and the new near Farmer's Bridge

The Black Country Museum is situated at the mouth of the Dudley Tunnel near Tipton Junction. This offers a fascinating insight into life and industry of bygone times. This is achieved by very clever reconstruction and is so lifelike that it gives very much more than just a glimpse of the past.

Ride 8

The Kingswinford Branch Railway Path, Castlecroft to Wall Heath

A surprisingly rural industrial trail along a magnificent recreational railway path.

Maps: Landranger 1:50000 series. Sheet number 139

Distance: Total length of railway path to cycling standards 5½miles (9 km). Return trip 11 miles (18 km).

Waymarked: Yes

Gradients: An easy, flat cycle path.

Surface: Almost perfect for gentle cycling. Mostly consolidated gravel.

Future Proposals: This section links with an extension into Valley Park, Wolverhampton at its northern end. At the southern end, the old Kingswinford Railway links with the old Pensnett Railway, but the two lines are at different levels. Some road bridges have also been removed on the Pensnett Railway but there are tentative plans to upgrade this section.

Shops and Refreshments: There are numerous access points, all of which are close to shops, pubs and other facilities.

Special Warnings: N/A

Permits: N/A

This recreational railway path is built on the old trackbed of the Kingswinford railway which was built partly as a colliery railway in about 1860. It was then extended between 1912 and 1925, as part of the Great Western Railway's holdings, to join up with the main Worcester to Wolverhampton line. After nationalisation the railway found itself under the management of British Railways (Western Region), but due to declining use it was closed under the Beeching cuts. The last train ran along the line on the 24th June 1965.

The line was open to passenger traffic for only the first seven years after its inception, but was never a commercial success. After 1933 only goods traffic used the line except for a few troop movements during World War ll. In the aftermath of the D-Day landings,

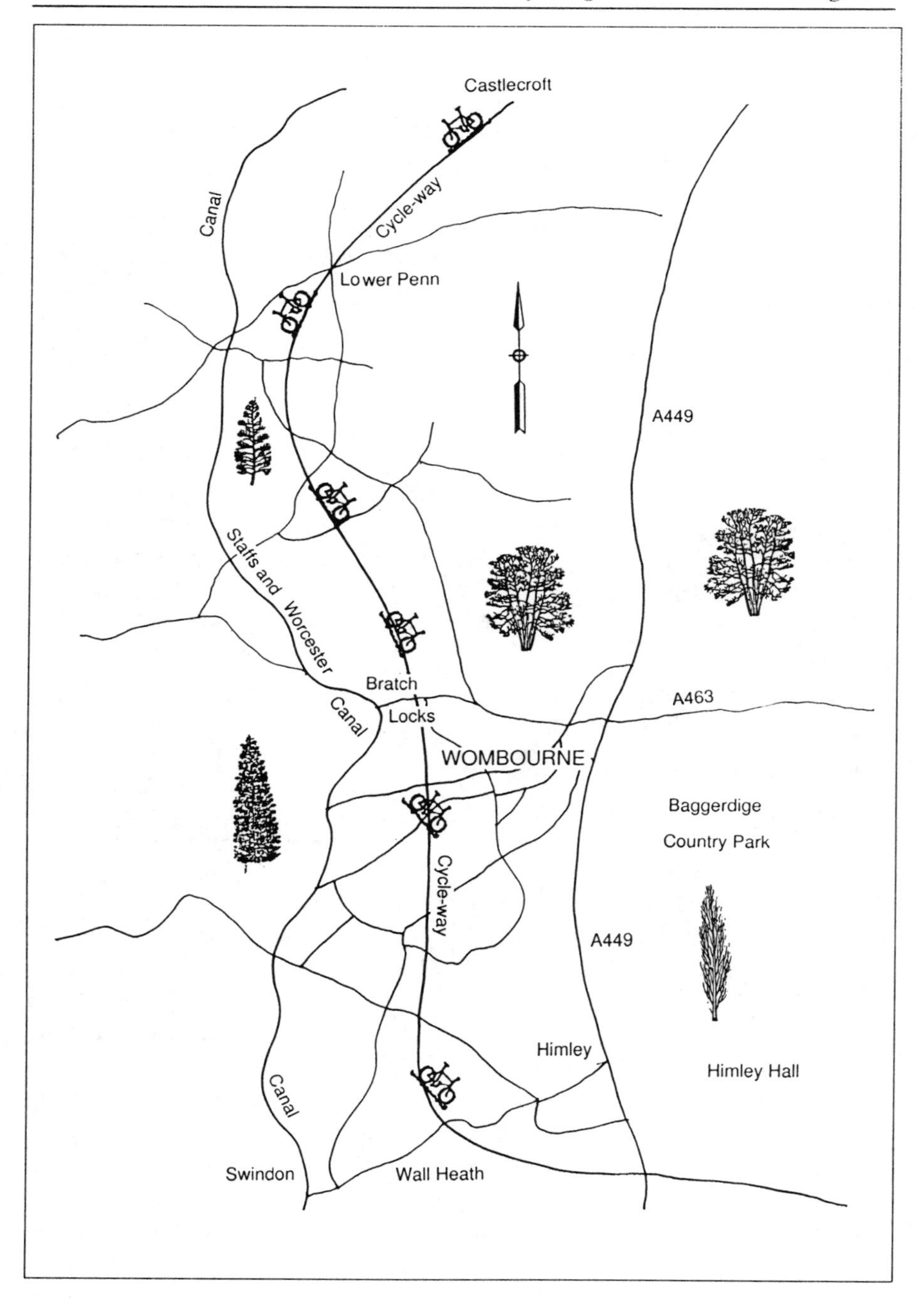

Castlecroft
Canal
Cycle-way
Lower Penn
A449
Staffs and Worcester
Canal
Bratch
Locks
A463
WOMBOURNE
Baggerdige
Country Park
Cycle-way
A449
Himley
Himley Hall
Canal
Swindon
Wall Heath

Near old Himley Station

the line served a particularly important purpose in ferrying wounded allied troops to local hospitals in the area.

Today the trackbed of the old line remains to serve a very useful purpose for the local community by offering a first class opportunity to get out into the wilds without having to travel miles away from the area. Walkers, horse riders, cyclists and nature lovers all benefit from this excellent recreational facility.

Access Points

There are plenty of excellent easy access points to the railway. Car parking is available at Himley plantation, which is situated between the villages of Himley and Swindon, just off the A449; at Old Wombourne Station, which can be found near the Bratch locks in Wombourne; and at Lower Penn, which is off the Langley Road south of Castlecroft.

The Route

No specific instructions are needed. Once you have joined the railway path at any of the above mentioned access points, simply head off in whichever direction takes your fancy and enjoy the easy, traffic- free cycling. There are a few well-positioned map boards which will clearly indicate your position at any given point.

Nearby

The Bratch Waterworks is a superb example of the brash, Victorian Gothic architecture which gives so much character to this area. It opened in 1897 with two wonderful steam engines which were affectionately known as Victoria and Alexandra. These vast engines required large amounts of coal which was brought up to the site by the nearby Staffordshire and Worcester Canal. The waterworks lost much of its appeal when it was converted to electric power in 1960.

Along the railway path you will have the opportunity to see a vast array of varied wildlife. As well as mice, voles, weasels and stoats, you are quite likely to glimpse a fox or a badger, especially during the very early morning or late evening. Birds which have settled in the environment include graceful sparrow hawks and kestrels as well as several species of owl.

Ride 9

Baggeridge Country Park and Bratch Locks

A ride out of Baggeridge Country Park near Dudley forming a rural circuit via Bratch Locks and Himley Hall.

Maps: Landranger 1:50000 series. Sheet number 139

Distance: 12 miles (19 km)

Waymarked: No

Gradients: Few climbs

Surface: A mixture of lanes, country park roads and canal towing-path

Future Proposals: N/A

Shops and Refreshments: Plenty of shops and pubs along the way

Special Warnings: Baggeridge Country Park and Himley Hall do not allow large parties of cyclists and discourage cycling away from their main access roads.

Permits: A British Waterways permit is required to ride along the canal towing-path.

This route makes the best of some of this area's most fascinating and attractive features by combining them into one delightfully simple and rewarding cycle ride. Starting out and finishing at Baggeridge Country Park, this route goes via country lanes, the towing-path of the Staffordshire and Worcester Canal, Bratch Locks and Himley Hall. None of it is too strenuous, all of it is interesting and most of it avoids traffic completely thus making an ideal route for family groups.

Baggeridge Country Park and Himley Hall share an interesting history. Baggeridge Country Park offers public access to 62 hectares (152 acres) of parkland which previously formed the northern sector of the former Himley Hall Estate. This estate had been in the ownership of the Lords of Dudley since the Domesday book, although the family only took up residence in Himley Hall in 1750 after Dudley Castle, their formal residence, had been ravaged by fire. The estate was originally landscaped by Capability Brown, but his work was doomed when coal was discovered under the site in the

On the towing-path

late nineteenth century. By 1912 Baggeridge Colliery was in full production and employed 3000 men. After a slow decline the colliery was closed in the late 1960s and was left to fall into dereliction. In the early 1970s the derelict land was purchased by the local authority which began the long job of reclamation. Between 1970, when it was designated a country park, and 1983, when most work was completed, over 20,000 trees and shrubs were planted and over 375,000 cubic metres of earth were moved.

Access Points

Baggeridge Country Park is situated off the A463. It is clearly signposted and there is good car parking available.

The Route

1. From the car park of Baggeridge Country Park, take the main driveway back towards the main A463. Turn right along the A463 and after a very short distance turn left into Penn Road, signposted to Upper Penn.

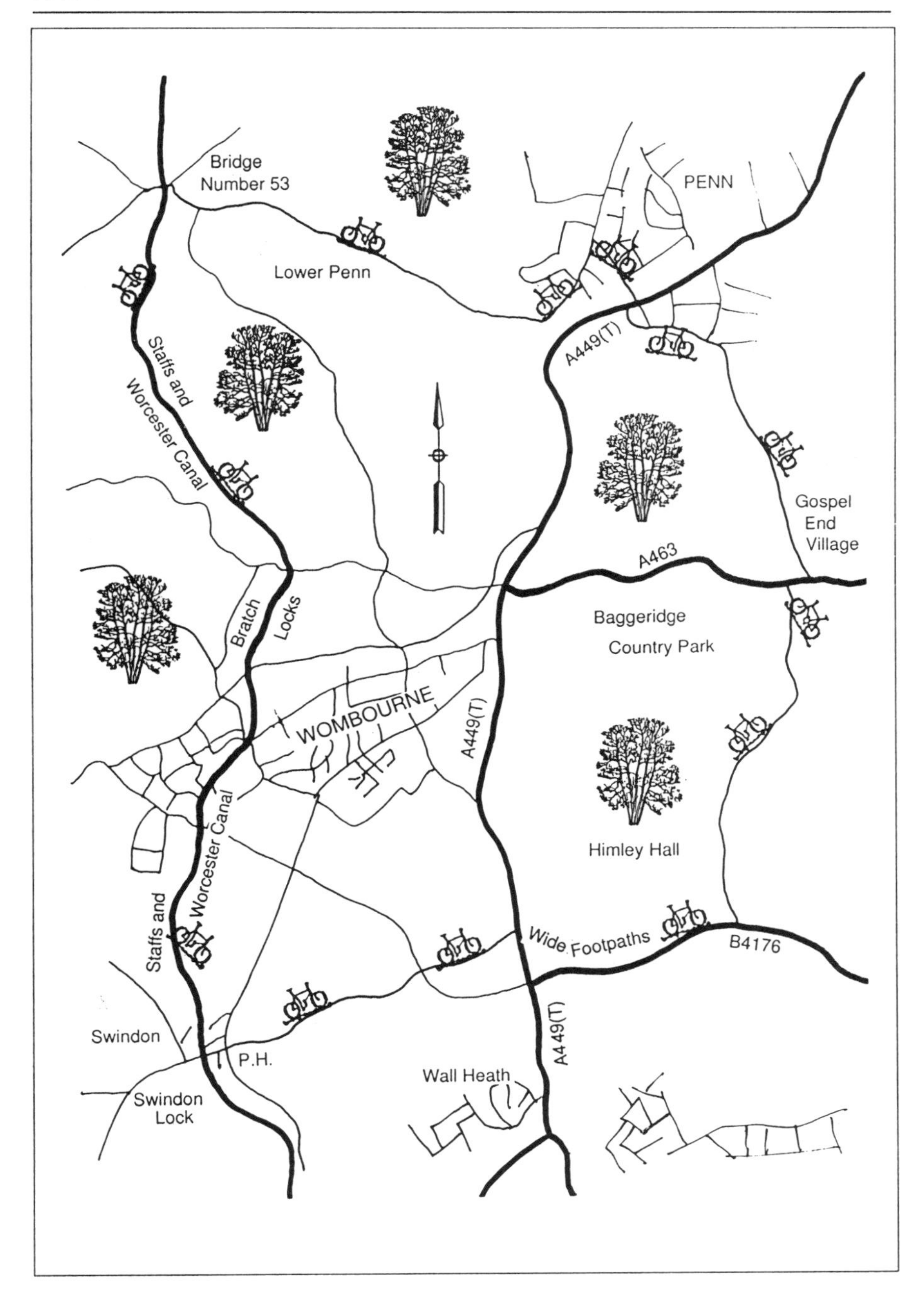
Bridge
Number 53
PENN
Lower Penn
Staffs and
Worcester Canal
A449(T)
Gospel
End
Village
A463
Bratch
Locks
Baggeridge
Country Park
WOMBOURNE
A449(T)
Himley Hall
Worcester Canal
Staffs and
Wide Footpaths
B4176
Swindon
P.H.
Swindon
Lock
Wall Heath
A449(T)

2. After passing the golf course at Penn Common and coming into the edge of the village, turn left by the church into Vicarage Road.
3. At the traffic lights go straight on into Hollybush Lane.
4. At the T-junction with Warstones Road, turn left.
5. After half a mile turn right up Springhill Lane.
6. After just over a mile, carry straight on at the crossroads, following the signs for Seisdon. Keep straight on until you arrive at a T-junction by a canal bridge.
7. This is bridge number 53 of the Staffordshire and Worcestershire Canal. Go left along the towing-path (heading due south).
8. Continue along the towing-path past the descending Bratch staircase locks to Swindon Lock (by the concrete bridge).
9. Turn left along the road by Swindon Lock and follow it around as the road bends left by The Old Bush public house.
10. Immediately after the car park of the public house, turn right into Himley Lane. Continue under the old railway bridge which now carries the Kingswinford Railway Path (see description in Ride 8).
11. At the end of Himley Lane, at the T-junction with the B4176 Bridgnorth to Dudley Road, carry straight on through the bollards into the route for pedestrians and cycles only. Join the extended part of Himley Lane.
12. At the end of Himley Lane turn right along School Road.
13. At the end of School Road turn right along the main A449. This is a very busy road but there is a suitable footpath on the far side which would be safer for cycles. After a very short distance turn left at the traffic lights onto the B4176.
14. A short distance along the B4176, turn left into Himley Hall and go north along the estate access roads to return to Baggeridge Country Park.

Nearby

Bratch Locks is a glorious spot and a good place to sit on a sunny day and watch pleasure boaters working their way up and down the canal past the old toll house. It is amazing how many theories there are on the proper way to work these locks, although most people settle for the advice of the resident experts. The pounds between the locks are much shorter than usual, the head water being stored in side pounds. This shortage of water can sometimes cause problems and it is not uncommon to see boats aground in the pounds.

Originally, Bratch Locks was built as a three lock staircase (with no separating pounds) which rose through thirty feet in very little forward distance compared with conventional locks. The unconventional side pounds were a later addition which considerably increased the speed of the two-way traffic flow.

Ride 10

Cycling in The Wyre Forest

A great cycling facility in the forest near Kidderminster and Bewdley.

Maps: Landranger 1:50000 series. Sheet number 139

Distance: Over 5 miles (8 km) of lorry track in the main forest block and many miles of off-road trail here and in the North Kinlet forest block.

Waymarked: The lorry tracks and bridleways are marked in strategic places and are easy to follow.

Gradients: Plenty of ups and downs. The lorry tracks are fairly easy going.

Surface: The hard base stone of the gravelled lorry tracks means they are usually easily passable, even in wet weather. Some of the trails in North Kinlet can be very hard going in the wet and tend to be dangerously slippery in places.

Future Proposals: N/A

Shops and Refreshments: Forest visitor centre off the A456

Special Warnings: Always take proper safety precautions when rough riding and if you are alone, make sure someone knows where you have gone. Head protection essential for serious off-road forays.

Permits: N/A

The modern Wyre Forest takes its name from the medieval royal hunting ground which was known as the Forest of Wyre. The forest not only offers a spectacular display of ever changing woodland, but also teems with wildlife including the shy fallow deer. Within the nearby Severn Valley is the lovely old town of Bewdley and the famous Severn Valley Steam Railway which has formed the location or background scenery of many well-known film shoots.

Within the forest there are great cycling opportunities for all aspects of leisure cycling, and challenging mountain bike trails for experts and beginners alike. There are many miles of safe, traffic-free lorry tracks for hours of simple cycling pleasure in beautiful surroundings.

Forest Enterprise has given a great deal of thought to its cycling policy in the Wyre Forest and has come up with an excellent solution. The net result is that all types of leisure cycling can be enjoyed in the forest without causing any undue disturbance to walkers, horse riders or other forest users. Horse riding is catered for under a separate provision and it should be noted that waymarks with horseshoe symbols do not indicate that cycling is allowed, unless they are along a gravelled roadway. Walkers have their own specific routes which normally utilise the narrower trails, and the working activity of the forest is invariably well marked with appropriate warning signs.

Access Points

The visitor centre is situated off the A456, approached from the east via the Bewdley bypass. Start here for cycling on the lorry tracks of the main Wyre forest block.

The Wyre Forest Visitor Centre

The North Kinlet car park is situated off the B4194, just north-west of Bewdley. Start here for rough riding and mountain biking in the North Kinlet block.

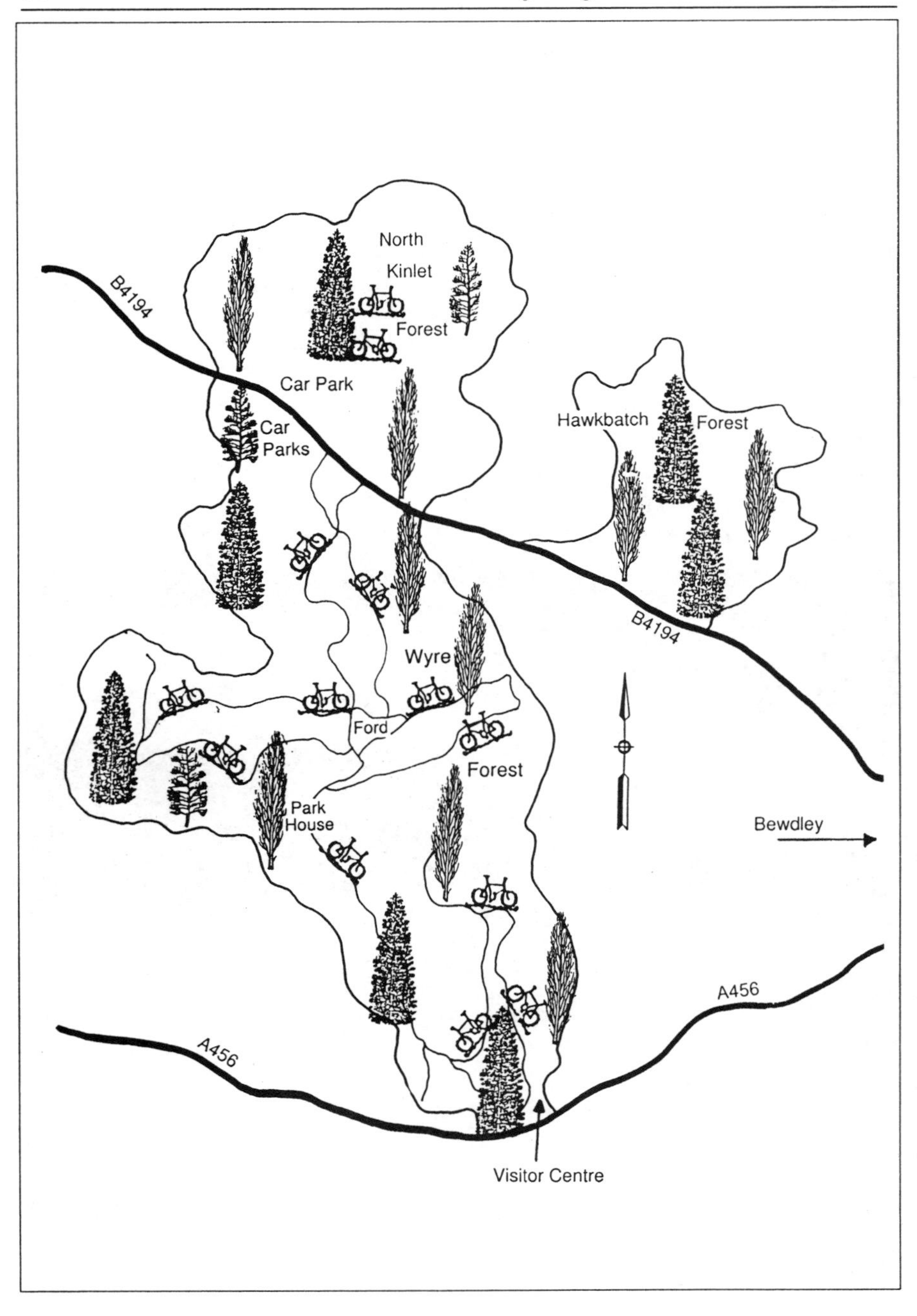
North
Kinlet
Forest
B4194
Car Park
Car
Parks
Hawkbatch
Forest
B4194
Wyre
Ford
Forest
Park
House
Bewdley
A456
A456
Visitor Centre

The Route

For cycling purposes The Wyre Forest can be conveniently sub-divided into three sections, each with its own cycling policy. In the main forest block, known as the Wyre Main Block, cycling is allowed along the forestry gravel/lorry tracks and public bridleways. In the North Kinlet forest block, north of the B4194, the cycling policy is on a go-as-you-please basis and is, therefore, ideally suited to rough riding expeditions. In the last small forestry block, known as Hawkbatch and separate from the other two blocks, cycling is not encouraged. Whichever forest block you choose to explore, a compass is a desirable, if not an essential, aid, not so much for point to point navigation as there are always several ways between any two points, but more for general trend navigation.

If you simply want to enjoy a great cycling experience in the forest, just set out from the main visitor centre area, head north into the main forest block and try to make your way to the B4194 and return. You could easily take two to three hours or even longer over this route. Don't forget to make provision if sandwiches and drinks are on your agenda, you won't find any shops in the forest.

For those who want to try their hand at pure mountain biking/rough riding, start from the North Kinlet car park which is situated off the B4194, north west of Bewdley. From here there are several trails and tracks which will lead you north and east into the heart of this forest block.

Nearby

If you want to journey back in time to the glorious days of the great steam railways, visit The Severn Valley Steam Railway. It routes for some 16 miles through the glorious Severn Valley and calls at many town and village stops along the way. There is a station on the edge of Bewdley and there are cycle racks at the various stations. Cycles can be carried only with specific permission of the staff or guard.

On the edge of Bewdley is the Bewdley Safari Park. If you are travelling by car there are over 160 wild species and exotic animals within the confines of this 200 acre park, but definitely no cycling here!

Ride 11

Stourport to Bewdley

An up and down rural ride with great views over the Severn Valley.

Maps: Landranger 1:50000 series. Sheet number 139

Distance: 11 miles (18 km)

Waymarked: No

Gradients: A couple of sharp climbs and one steep descent

Surface: Tarmac country lanes

Future Proposals: N/A

Shops and Refreshments: A wide choice of pubs, cafés, restaurants and shops in Stourport and Bewdley

Special Warnings: N/A

Permits: N/A

This is a delightfully easy return ride along quiet, minor roads alongside and above the River Severn. There are a couple of sharp climbs, but in return for your efforts there are some fantastic views along the Severn Valley and one breathtakingly fast descent. The traffic levels are normally very slight and the topography of the valley offers very good shelter from prevailing winds.

In Stourport on Severn there is a permanent riverside amusements park, steamer rides on the river, rowing boat hire and children's play areas. As well as all this, there is a fascinating canal basin and a good central shopping area. In Bewdley, if you have time, visit the museum, which is housed in an 18th century butcher's shambles. There are excellent displays and demonstrations which explain in some detail the intricacies of clay pipe-making, rope-making and other fascinating local crafts. Tucked away behind the museum are the tranquil Queen Elizabeth ll Jubilee Gardens.

The places of interest in Stourport and Bewdley, and the added attraction of the River Severn, make this ride an ideal full day's

The River Severn in Bewdley

expedition. There are first class facilities for eating and drinking in both towns, as well as several out-of-town establishments.

Access Points

The starting point of this ride is from the car park of the Riverside Country Park, behind the municipal buildings in Stourport. There is good car parking here. A good alternative starting point is from the eastern side of the river in Severn Side South, just off the centre of Bewdley.

The Route

1. From the car park of the Riverside Country Park in Stourport, head out of the access past the municipal buildings and go right, towards the town.
2. At the first junction turn right and cross the River Severn on the main A451 road bridge.
3. Shortly after crossing the river, turn right – signposted to Areley Kings Church.

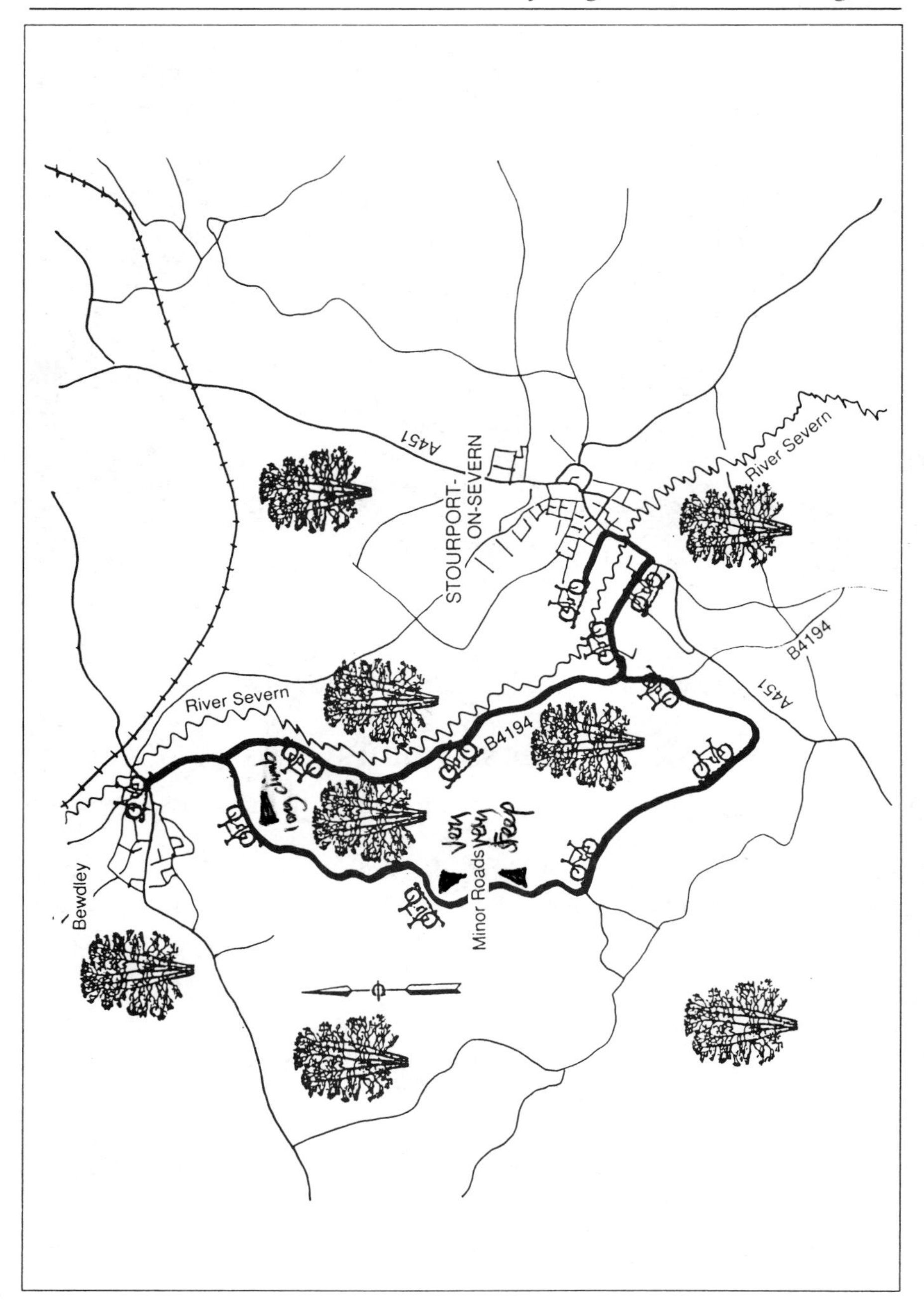
Bewdley
River Severn
STOURPORT-ON-SEVERN
A451
River Severn
B4194
B4194
A451
Minor Roads
Long climb
Very very steep

4. At a T-junction of the B4194 turn left, signposted to Astley.
5. After a very short distance, take the unsigned road which forks off to the right.
6. After about three quarters of a mile, turn right at a T-junction and begin a fairly sharp climb.
7. At the next T-junction turn right and descend to a ford. Continue to follow the lane.
8. At the T-junction turn left and follow the B4194 for the short distance into Bewdley.
9. After exploring Bewdley, return to Stourport on the B4194 and past Areley Kings Church.

Nearby

Blackstone Meadows Country Park is a lovely waterside attraction located between the B4194 and the River Severn, on the way back from Bewdley to Stourport. The meadows give you good access to the beauty of the River Severn and offer an ideal picnic spot.

Ride 12

The Staffordshire and Worcester Canal

A long trip along the lovely towing-paths of the Staffordshire and Worcestershire Canal from Stourport-on-Severn to Autherley Junction near Wolverhampton.

Maps: Landranger 1:50000 series. Sheet numbers 138 and 139

Distance: One way – 25½ miles (41 km). Return – 51 miles (82 km)

Waymarked: Easy to follow route with bridge numbers, lock numbers and mileposts to help you along your way.

Gradients: None at all apart from lock rises of a few feet

Surface: A few muddy patches but generally the going is quite good. If in doubt, get off and push for a short distance. None of the soft or broken-down areas of towing-path are very long.

Future Proposals: British Waterways is constantly improving the towing-path.

Shops and Refreshments: Plenty of bridge exits along the way give access to towns and villages. There are also a fair number of canal-side pubs.

Special Warnings: Beware of mooring spikes and mooring ropes.

Permits: British Waterways permit required.

When the Staffordshire and Worcestershire Canal was originally planned, James Brindley laid out a route which joined the River Severn at an obscure hamlet called Lower Milton. This location was chosen because it was the point where the little River Stour flowed into the big River Severn. Thus, when the canal was built in 1772, the new town of Stourport was born. It was the first canal-based boom town. The nucleus of Stourport was the basin where the canal locked down into the River Severn. It was here that the canal narrow boats transferred their cargoes into larger river barges (Severn Trows) which were more suited for the ongoing journey South West and to the turbulence of the river waters.

In the 1960s modern Stourport seemed to grow apart from its true origins and gave the impression that it had re-centred itself on the river bridges, paying little heed to the existence of the canal to which it owed its very existence. In recent times, however, the canal and the canal basin have been freshened up and appear to have once again been granted the respect and status that they deserve.

This section of the Staffordshire and Worcestershire Canal forms a link between Stourport on The River Severn and the Northern Birmingham Canal Navigations (BCN) junction with the Shropshire Union Canal at Autherley Junction. From here the Staffordshire and Worcestershire Canal continues north to join the Trent and Mersey at Great Haywood. This part of the network formed a vital part of a grand plan to create a water transport system joining three great English rivers: the Severn, the Trent and the Mersey. Many waterway commentators consider this stretch of canal to be one of the prettiest parts of the whole system. Its most memorable features are perhaps the deep and narrow cuttings which form the character of the western part of this section. Unfortunately, they also create narrow towing-paths which are not the best for cycling purposes but quite passable with patience.

Access Points

Start at bridge 4 of the Staffordshire and Worcestershire Canal, York Street, Stourport at the northern end of the canal basin. Alternatively, try Autherley Junction, the junction of the Shropshire Union Canal and The Staffordshire and Worcestershire Canal, Staffordshire, north of Wolverhampton, east of the A449(T). A-Z reference: P19 2F

Obviously the canal can also be accessed by virtually any bridge along its route.

The Route

1. On the towpath of The Staffordshire and Worcestershire Canal, with your back to bridge number 4, the canal on your left, proceed straight on along the towing-path and past the ascending York Street lock.
2. After half a mile, pass under a railway.
3. After two miles you will pass Falling Sands Lock.
4. After bridge number twelve pass ascending Caldwall Lock.

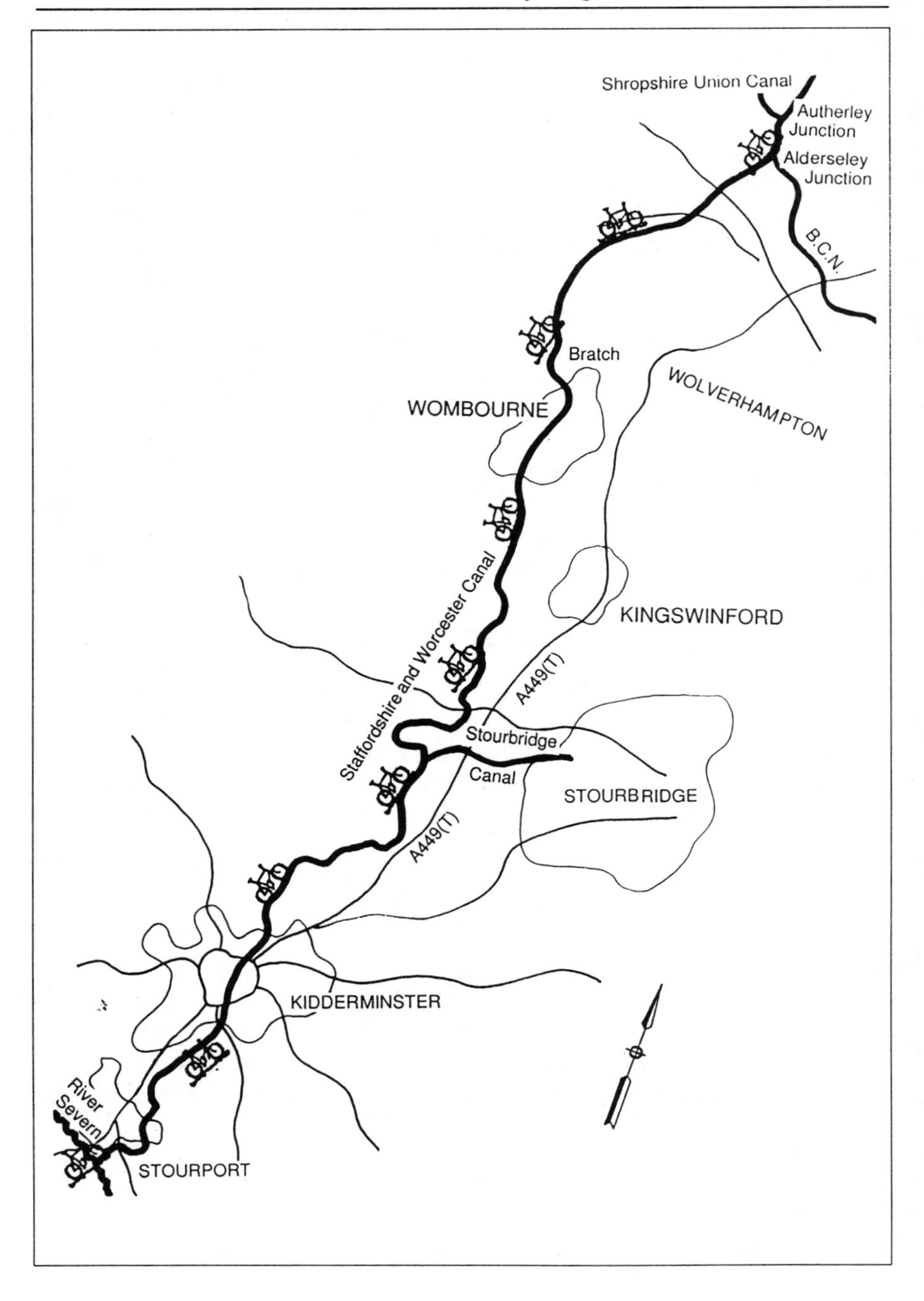
Shropshire Union Canal
Autherley Junction
Alderseley Junction
B.C.N.
Bratch
WOMBOURNE
WOLVERHAMPTON
Staffordshire and Worcester Canal
KINGSWINFORD
A449(T)
Stourbridge
Canal
STOURBRIDGE
A449(T)
KIDDERMINSTER
River Severn
STOURPORT

5. The towing-path crosses over to the left at bridge number 16. The water should now be on your right.
6. After six miles you arrive at bridge number 20, the B4189. Go right here for the public house.
7. After bridge number 22 and ascending Debdale Lock, pass through the short Cookley Tunnel.
8. At about 8½ miles pass under bridge number 26 near Caunsall village.
9. After a further two miles, pass bridge number 28 near Kinver village.
10. After another mile, after passing bridge number 30 and ascending Hyde Lock, you will pass through the short Dunsley Tunnel.
11. At twelve miles, after passing under bridge number 32, the A458, and passing the ascending Stewponey Lock, pass under bridge number 33 opposite Stourton Junction with the Stourbridge Canal and the BCN.
12. After bridge number 35, pass ascending Gothersley and Rocky Locks.
13. After about 15 miles you will find a pleasant public house by bridge number 37 and Greensforge Lock.
14. After 17 miles you will pass bridge number 41 and the ascending Marsh lock.
15. After another half mile you will pass bridge number 42 and the ascending Botterham Staircase locks.
16. At about 18 miles, pass under the B4176.
17. After about 19 miles pass under bridge number 45 by Wombourne village.
18. At about 20 miles, after passing bridge number 47, ascend the Bratch Locks. The towing-path crosses over to go right at bridge number 47. The water should now be on your left.
19. After passing bridge number 49, ascend Awbridge Lock.
20. After passing bridge number 51, ascend Ebstree Lock.
21. After passing bridge number 52, ascend Dimmingsdale Lock.

The towing-path crosses over to the left, and the water should now be on your right.

22. At about 23 miles, after passing bridge number 58, ascend Wightwick Mill Lock.
23. After about another half mile, pass under bridge number 60 near Compton village. After passing bridge number 60, ascend Compton Lock.
24. At about 24 miles pass under a railway.
25. At just under 25 miles, pass opposite Aldersley Junction (with the Birmingham Canal at bridge number 64). Cross bridge number 64.
26. After 25½ miles arrive at Autherley Junction. On your left you will see the start of the Shropshire Union Canal.
27. If you wish to continue and link up with the Birmingham to Wolverhampton route, turn right at Autherley Junction. After about half a mile you will arrive at Aldersley Junction (see Ride 7).

Stourton Junction

Nearby

Kidderminster is a busy and industrious town which has been the leading carpet-weaving centre of the Midlands since Flemish influences in the 13th century. The modern industry is largely the brainchild of John Broom who invested vast sums to develop a carpet loom which was installed in Pearsall's factory in 1735. An excellent museum has a working example of John Broom's loom and a sample of the carpet that it was able to produce.

Kinver is a pretty village overlooked by an old Norman church. It is a good place to stop for a pub lunch. Kinver Edge is an excellent viewing point. Holy Austin Rock is a strange rock house on the hill.

Ride 13

The Clent Hills

A semi-rural ride from the base of the Clent Hills.

Maps: Landranger 1:50000 series. Sheet number 139

Distance: 24 miles (38.5 km)

Waymarked: No

Gradients: A few ups and downs along the route but nothing too daunting

Surface: Tarmac country lanes

Future Proposals: N/A

Shops and Refreshments: Plenty of pubs and village shops along the route

Special Warnings: N/A

Permits: N/A

This ride starts and finishes at the foot of the Clent Hills and explores some of the lovely villages and countryside to the south-west of Hagley and north-west of Bromsgrove. There is some lovely unspoilt scenery in the Clent Hills and some information on this can be obtained from the good local information boards and local tourism offices. The hills are largely in the care of the National Trust and rise to a height of 1035 feet above sea level. They are a very popular local attraction and can be quite busy on sunny weekends.

This is a very pleasant rural ride which offers a few steady climbs and a great variation of scenery. There are plenty of good stopping off places for food and drink and some of the views, especially around the Clent Hills, are memorable.

Access Points

To find Adam's Hill car park (OS sheet 139: 927 798), go into Clent village and with your back to St Leonard's Church, go up the hill into the more minor road opposite. After about half a mile, turn right up Mount Lane. Continue straight ahead for the car park.

The Route

1. From Adam's Hill car park in Clent Hills country park (see access points), by the Hill Tavern, the Four Stones restaurant and the cafe, turn down the hill, away from the car park.
2. After a few metres, take the left fork into Mount Hill, still going downhill and heading west.
3. At the bottom of Mount Lane, after about a quarter of a mile, go left at the T-junction.
4. At the crossroads by the Church of St Leonard's, after a total of about half a mile, turn right along Church Avenue, signposted to Belbroughton.
5. After crossing under the main A491, go straight on at the next junction, opposite the public house, onto the Belbroughton Road (straight ahead and forking to the left of the pub).
6. In the village of Belbroughton, carry straight on along the High Street, signposted to Blakedown and Chaddesley Corbett.
7. Take the second major left turn in the village to turn into Church Road, signposted to Broom Hill and Bournheath.
8. Follow the signposts to Woodcote through the hamlet of Broom Hill and then follow the signposted road to Catshill and Bromsgrove.
9. Continue to follow the road signposted to Bromsgrove until you arrive at a crossroads by a public house. Here take the right turn into Yarnold Lane to head west towards Dodford.
10. At the T-junction with Warbage Lane, turn right, signposted to Dodford and Belbroughton.
11. After just a few metres, turn left into Priory Road.
12. After passing a school, at a T-junction turn right into Fockbury Road, signposted to Bromsgrove.
13. At the main A448 crossroads, go straight ahead into Bungay Lane.
14. At the T-junction, turn right into Timberhonger Lane, signposted to Droitwich.
15. At the T-junction at the end of Timberhonger Lane, turn right, signposted to Kidderminster.

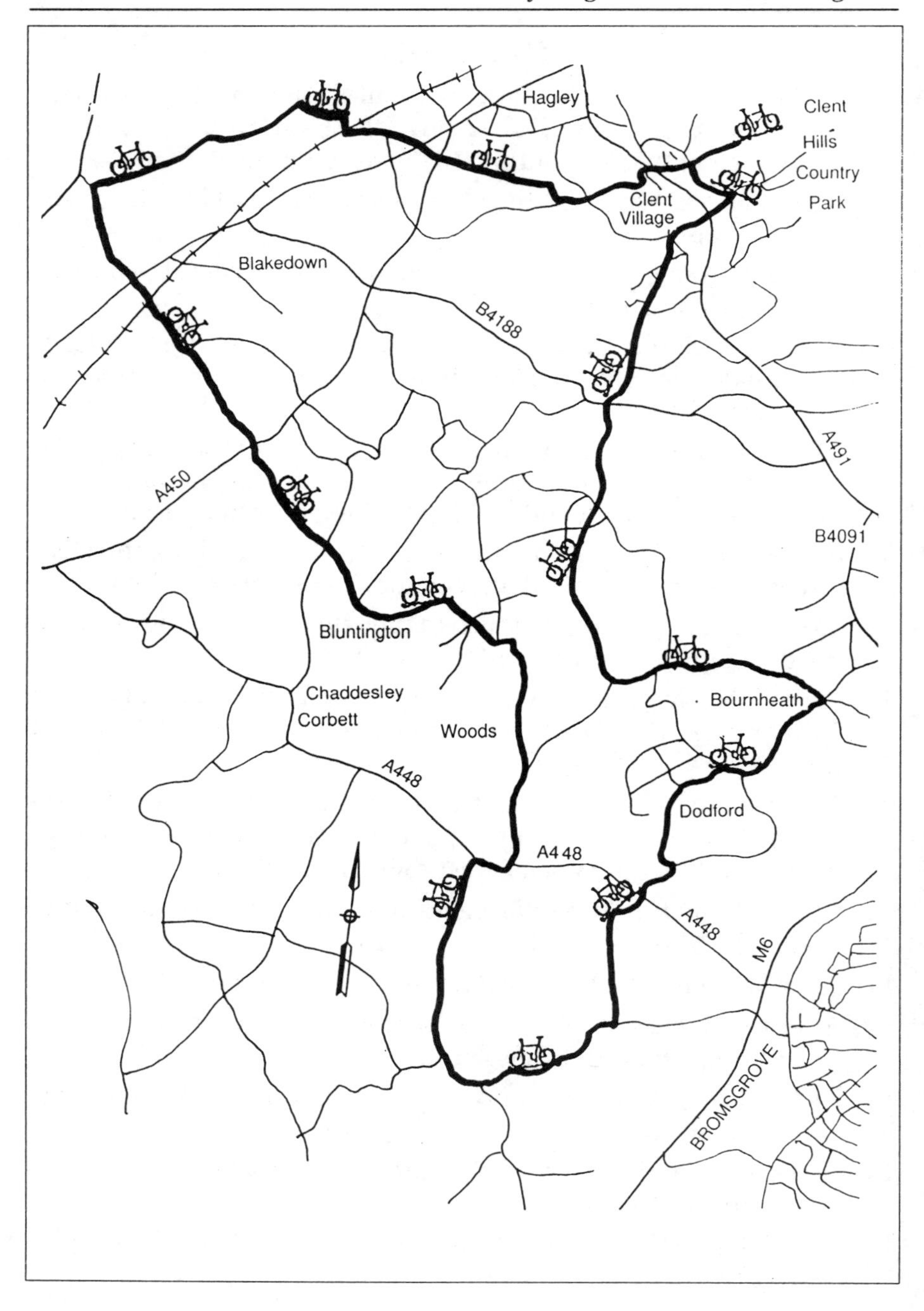
Hagley
Clent
Hills
Country
Park
Clent
Village
Blakedown
B4188
A491
A450
B4091
Bluntington
Chaddesley
Corbett
Woods
Bournheath
A448
Dodford
A4 48
A448
M6
BROMSGROVE

16. Turn right along the main A448 and after just a very short distance, turn left, signposted to Belbroughton.
17. In the hamlet of Woodcote Green, fork left into Woodcote Green Lane, signposted to Bluntington and Woodrow. Follow the road signposted to Bluntington through shady woodland.
18. At the village of Bluntington, go straight ahead at the crossroads. The road is signposted to Woodrow and Stourbridge.
19. At the crossroads with the A450, go straight over the A450 into the quiet lane opposite.
20. At the crossroads with the A456, cross the dual carriageway with care and go straight ahead into the lane opposite.
21. At the T-junction with Waggon Lane, turn right.
22. At the end of Waggon Lane, turn left towards Churchill.
23. At the T-junction in Churchill, turn right, signposted to Broom and Hagley.
24. After passing under the railway, at the T-junction, go straight ahead, crossing the main A456 into Thicknall Lane.
25. After a short distance, cross the next main road (the A450) to go straight ahead again into Thicknall Lane (the road marked as unsuitable for heavy goods vehicles). At this point you are on the outer edges of Hagley.
26. At the T-junction, go left, signposted to Clent.
27. At the island, take the second exit, signposted to Clent Hills. After a short distance you will arrive at a crossroads, go straight ahead into Adams Hill, leaving the public house on the right-hand side.
28. Follow Adams Hill up to the starting point at the foot of the upper hills.

Nearby

There are some great off-road mountain biking opportunities in the Clent Hills (access from Adam's Hill car park). Obey any signs prohibiting cycling and you will not go far wrong.

Ride 14

Mountain bike trails in the Lickey Hills

Some great mountain bike trails in the trees of the Lickey Hills.

Maps: Landranger 1:50000 series. Sheet number 139

Distance: Approximately 3½ miles (5.5 km)

Waymarked: Green Waymarker Posts

Gradients: Plenty to challenge even the most hardened enthusiast.

Surface: Muddy trails

Future Proposals: N/A

Shops and Refreshments: Visitor centre

Special Warnings: N/A

Permits: N/A

Although the routes are short, the Lickey Hills provide good, traffic-free mountain bike trails suitable for general rough riding or for the dedicated mountain biker. Sometimes the routes can be hard going and slippery, especially in rainy conditions, but they are challenging and very easily accessible.

Although small by many standards, the Lickey Hills Country Park offers a welcome diversion from the busy pace of the city. The bird life of the Lickey Hills is prolific, and as well as the waymarked cycle routes, there are a range of lovely waymarked walks and a free-to-enter visitor centre with masses of information and interpretation of the area.

Access Points

There is a visitor centre and a good car park at the Lickey Hills Country Park.

The Route

No special instructions are needed here. From the Lickey Hills visitor centre simply follow Green Waymarker Posts. A leaflet is normally available from the visitor centre.

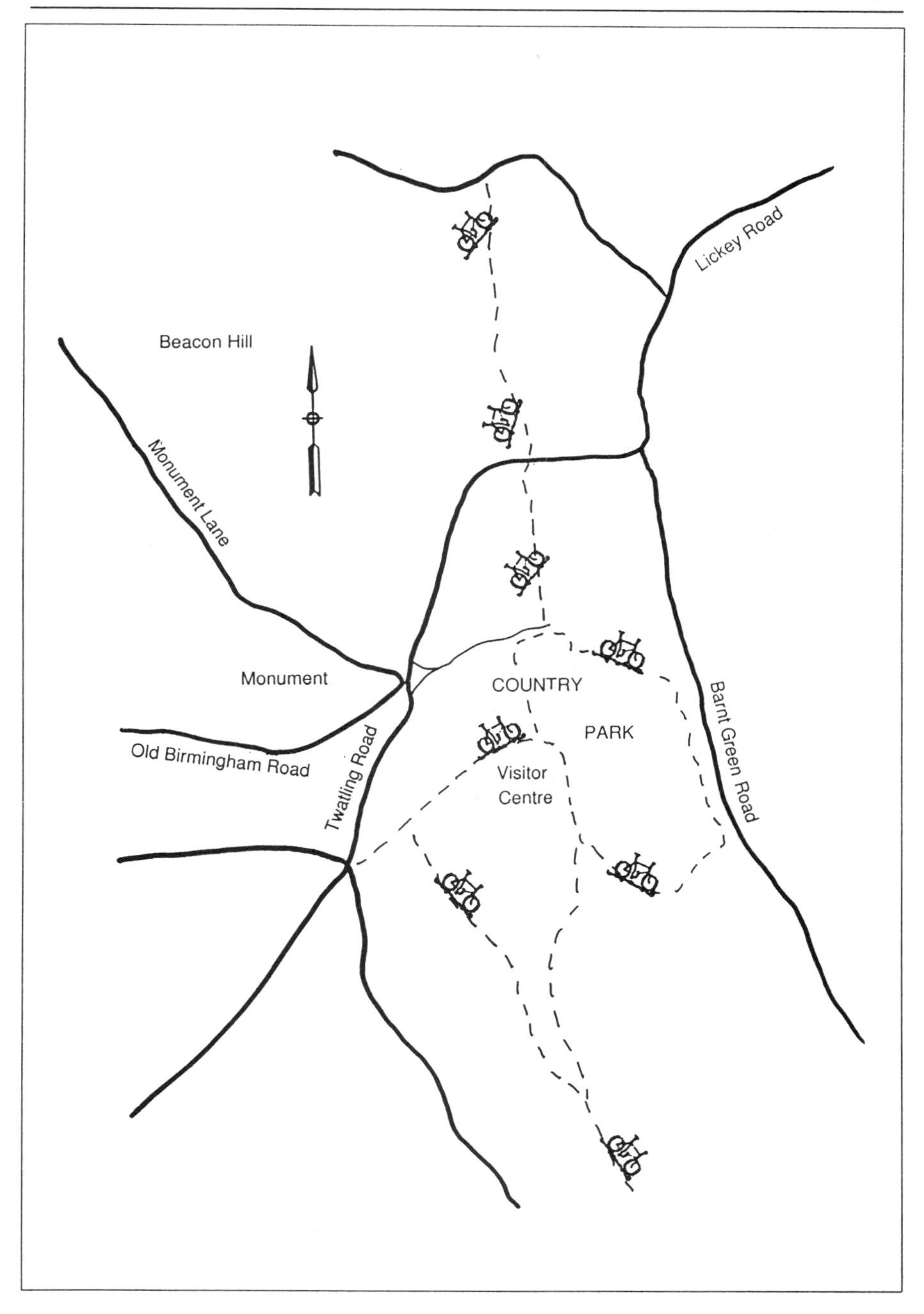
Lickey Road
Beacon Hill
Monument Lane
Monument
COUNTRY
PARK
Barnt Green Road
Old Birmingham Road
Twatling Road
Visitor
Centre

Rough riding in the Lickey Hills

Nearby

Away from the main Lickey Hills waymarked routes, there are some other mountain biking opportunities around the Monument Lane area, a short distance to the west. Nature trails are marked in the Lickey Hills with blue and yellow posts. These are generally restricted to walkers only.

Ride 15

A tour from the Lickey Hills

A delightful rural ride east of Birmingham from the Lickey Hills.

Maps: Landranger 1:50000 series. Sheet number 139

Distance: 18 miles (29 km) return

Waymarked: No

Gradients: Minimal

Surface: Tarmac country lane

Future Proposals: N/A

Shops and Refreshments: Plenty of places along the way

Special Warnings: N/A

Permits: N/A

This is a delightful area of south Birmingham with a wealth of attractive countryside, pretty suburbs, sections of old canal and attractive villages. The riding is not too energetic, the only climbs being brief undulations in the local landscape as the ground lifts you up to enjoy an even finer view of the surrounding countryside. The route is described from the Lickey Hills Country Park.

Along the way, the ride takes in a stretch of Icknield Street, an old Roman road which, along this particular stretch, has become little more than a very minor country lane with hardly sufficient room to let two cars pass. A careful study of OS maps 139 and 150 or a glance at your road map will reveal the fuller picture of Icknield Street, which formed part of the Roman Empire's vast international communications infrastructure. It is strange to think that Roman legions once marched to and fro along this lonely and forgotten stretch of English country lane. It is interesting to note the contrast with Icknield Street's modern equivalent, the M42.

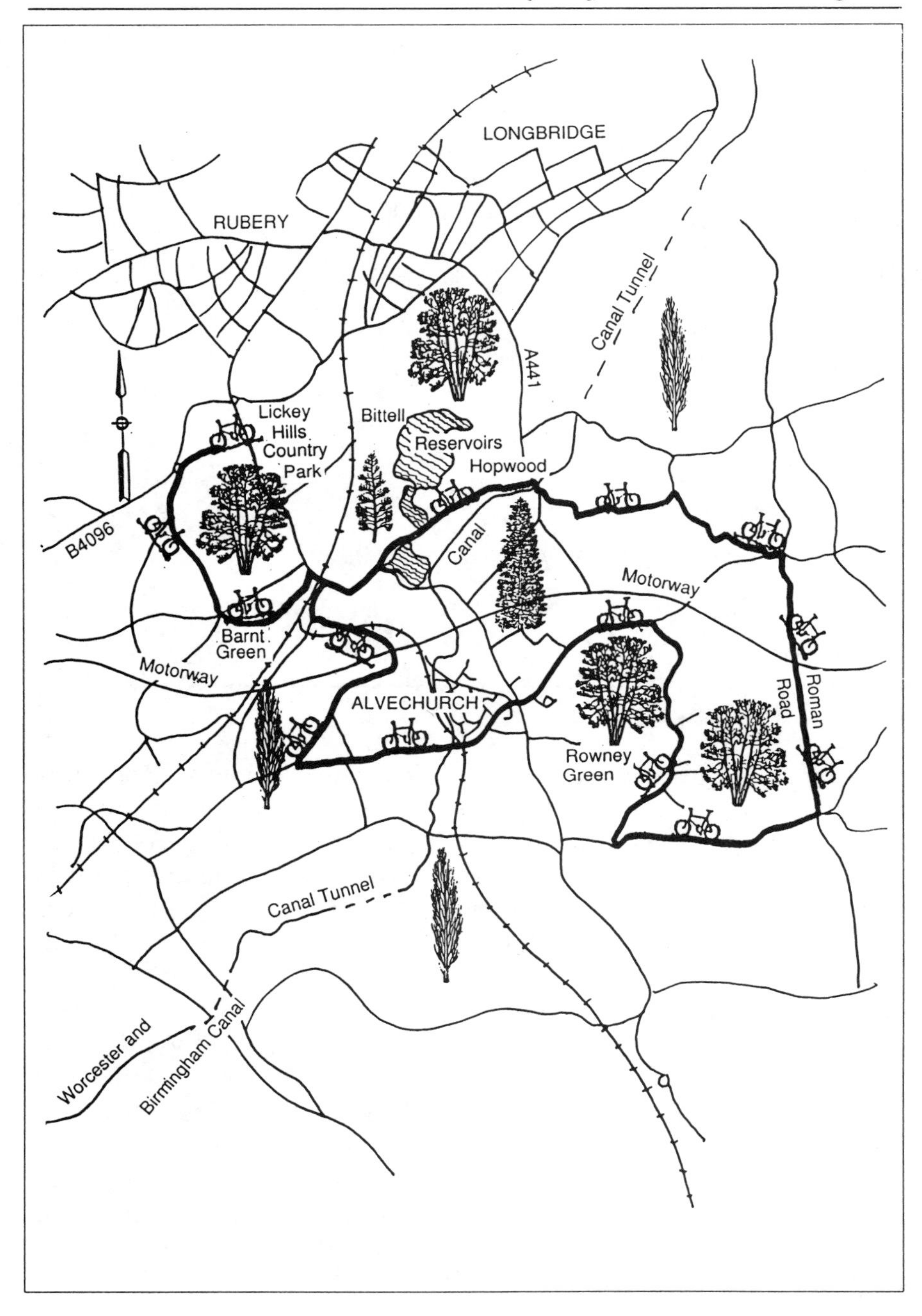
LONGBRIDGE
RUBERY
Canal Tunnel
A441
Lickey
Hills
Country
Park
Bittell
Reservoirs
Hopwood
B4096
Canal
Motorway
Barnt
Green
Motorway
ALVECHURCH
Rowney
Green
Road
Roman
Canal Tunnel
Worcester and
Birmingham Canal

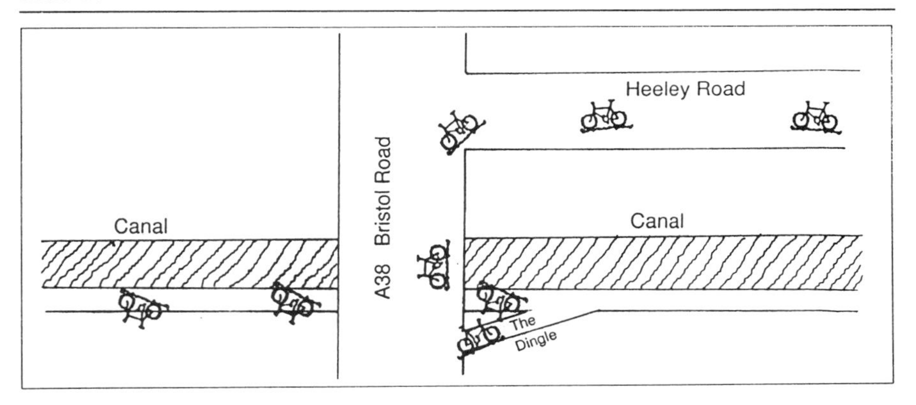

Access Points

There is a visitor centre and a good car park at the Lickey Hills Country Park.

The Route

1. From the Lickey Hills visitor centre, follow the made up road out of the car park.
2. Turn left, signposted to Barnt Green, and left at the next T-junction, towards Barnt Green Station.
3. After about two miles you will come to a T-junction with Kendal End Road to the left and Bittell Road to the right. Turn right along Bittell Road, cross under the railway and follow the signposts to Hopwood.
4. After about half a mile, where the road turns sharp right, keep left along Bittell Green Road and follow this road as it crosses Lower Bittell Reservoir to Hopwood.
5. At the T-junction with the A441 by the Worcester and Birmingham Canal(Birmingham Road to the left and Redditch Road to the right), turn right. Cross the canal and then turn immediately left into Ash Lane.
6. After about half a mile, turn left into Stonehouse Lane.
7. At the T-junction opposite a pretty, red brick cottage, turn right.
8. At the next T-junction, turn left and after a short distance, turn

right along Icknield Street (Roman road). Follow under the busy M42.

9. At the T-junction at the end of this section of the Roman Road, turn right by the grassy triangle.
10. After about one and a half miles, turn right into Rowney Green Lane, signposted to Rowney Green and Weatheroak.
11. After passing through Rowney Green village, you will come to a T-junction with Radford Road, go left here, signposted to Alvechurch.
12. In Alvechurch village, go left into the small square and then cross straight over the A441 to take the road towards the station.
13. Cross over the railway and the canal as you leave the village.
14. Just over a mile outside Alvechurch, turn right into Blackwell Road, signposted to Barnt Green and Birmingham.
15. Pass under the M42 motorway and continue into Barnt Green village. At the T-junction with Bittell Road turn left, signposted to Rednal. After passing under the railway, go left again into Fiery Hill Road to retrace your outbound route to return to the Lickey Hills Country Park.

Nearby

The delightful village of Alvechurch is a most interesting place to stop and explore. There are some fine and interesting little shops as well as some beautiful old buildings and welcoming pubs. On the western edge of the village is an excellent example of a meeting point of the old and the new (or newer). The old is the Worcester and Birmingham Canal and the new is the branch railway which runs from Barnt Green Junction south to Redditch and beyond.

The lovely little reservoirs of Upper Bittell and Lower Bittell act as header tanks to the Worcester and Birmingham Canal. From here the canal maintains its present level into Gas Street Basin in Birmingham by way of the 2726 metres long Kings Norton Tunnel. To the south the canal maintains its level by way of the 580 metres Tardebigge Tunnel. It then plummets down towards the Severn valley, initially by way of the thirty six lock Tardebigge flight.

Ride 16

Birmingham to Bournville

A ride along the canal to the chocolate factory in Bournville.

Maps: Landranger 1:50000 series. Sheet number 139

Distance: 16 miles (26 km) return

Waymarked: Well signed along the canal towing-path.

Gradients: No hills

Surface: Partly very well-surfaced canal towing-path, partly suburban streets and estate roads.

Future Proposals: N/A

Shops and Refreshments: Numerous pubs, shops and cafés

Special Warnings: N/A

Permits: A British Waterways cycling permit.

This fascinating trip will take you from the centre of Birmingham, along a very pleasant stretch of canal and then onto one of Birmingham's most famous and most successful industrial centres, the chocolate factory at Bournville. The ride starts out at Gas Street Basin on the Worcester and Birmingham Canal and progresses through Edgbaston Tunnel, where you should dismount for safety. The surface is good and the surroundings are fascinating; this is a very different way to see Birmingham.

Around the chocolate factory at Bournville you will have a chance to see the magnificent and innovative development which was carried out by the Cadbury brothers when Bournville was originally built. Take a little time to explore the garden suburb and appreciate the fine buildings and landscaping.

Access Points

Gas Street Basin/Farmer's Bridge Junction, Birmingham. There is good all day car parking here and the rail links could hardly be better. Alternatively you could start at Cadbury World and use the route to cycle into the centre of Birmingham.

Open spaces around Bournville, near the factory

The Route

1. From Gas Street Basin, which is on the Worcester and Birmingham Canal, facing the water, turn right.
2. After passing through Edgbaston tunnel and following the canal for about four miles, you will arrive at bridge number 80 on the Worcester and Birmingham Canal. The canal passes under Bristol Road, but you should take the pedestrian exit which will lead you up to Bristol Road via the little road known as "The Dingle".
3. Turn right out of "The Dingle" and onto Bristol Road to head back over the canal.
4. After crossing over the canal, turn right, under the railway bridge, into Heeley Road.
5. At the end of Heeley Road, after passing Selly Oak Station, turn right along Raddlebarn Road and then left along the modern estate road, Raddlebarn Farm Drive.
6. At the end of Raddlebarn Farm Drive you will find a pedestrian

Gas
Street
A38 Bristol Road
Pershore Road
Heeley Road
Estate
Canal
Roads
Cadbury
World
A38 Bristol Road

and cycle path. This will take you firstly, into another part of the estate road, and then (just keep following the obvious route) along another pedestrian and cycle path which will put you alongside the Worcester and Birmingham Canal on the opposite side to the main towing-path.

7. Here you follow the road signposted to Cadbury World. This will lead down from the canal into Bournville Lane.
8. Turn right along Bournville Lane and go through the tunnel under the railway and canal. Continue along Bournville Lane, past the chocolate factory to the T-junction.
9. Go right at the T-junction and you will see Cadbury World on your right.

Nearby

In 1879 George and Richard Cadbury, who were already well-established and respected chocolate makers and dedicated Quakers, moved their manufacturing into a new factory on the banks of a stream called Bournbrook, on the southern edge of Birmingham. They named their new factory Bournville. For their employees they built beautiful houses and created tree-lined avenues amid open lawns and superbly landscaped gardens. Not satisfied with simply building a superb garden suburb, the Cadbury brothers then bought two idyllic 14th century houses, Selly Manor and Minworth Greaves. They had these beautiful buildings carefully taken down from their original sites and transported piece by piece to the Bournville sites where they were meticulously re-built. All this effort was simply to give the new site a rural feel. This fantastic work is well preserved, making Bournville one of the most attractive residential areas of South Birmingham.

A visit to Cadbury World is a must for chocolate lovers and a potential disaster for slimmers. The displays take you from the South American rain forests where the cocoa was first grown, through the origins of the Cadbury empire to modern production line techniques. The experience is one of sight, sound, smell and taste, and a great treat for children of all ages!

Ride 17

The Rea Valley Cycle Route

A great traffic-free cycle route from the suburbs to the centre of Birmingham, and a great way to see one of the city's finest parks.

Maps: Landranger 1:50000 series. Sheet number 139

Distance: 5 miles (8 km) each way

Waymarked: Very clearly marked with blue signs

Gradients: Hardly any slopes

Surface: Nearly all tarmac, shared-use pathways

Future Proposals: To extend the route further out of the city and to incorporate new routes from the city centre hub

Shops and Refreshments: You are never far from shops or pubs.

Special Warnings: Bell needed to warn pedestrians

Permits: N/A

This eight kilometre cycleway is ideal for exercising and loosening up tired and underused muscles or for a day out in Birmingham with a difference. For commuters and shoppers it represents a superb way to get into and out of the city centre. The surface is first class for cycling and the gradients are slight. The route is entirely off main roads and the section through Cannon Hill Park, particularly, is a most pleasant ride in its own right.

The Rea Valley Route is a mixture of special features rather than a continuous unbroken path. Generally, from Cannon Hill Park northwards it utilises quiet, urban roads which have benefited from traffic control and calming initiatives. From Cannon Hill Park southwards towards Stirchley, it utilises shared-use foot and cycle paths with segregation and special bridges.

Access Points

There are dozens of points where you can join the route. In the south is Hazelwell Road, Stirchley, and at the northern extremity is the

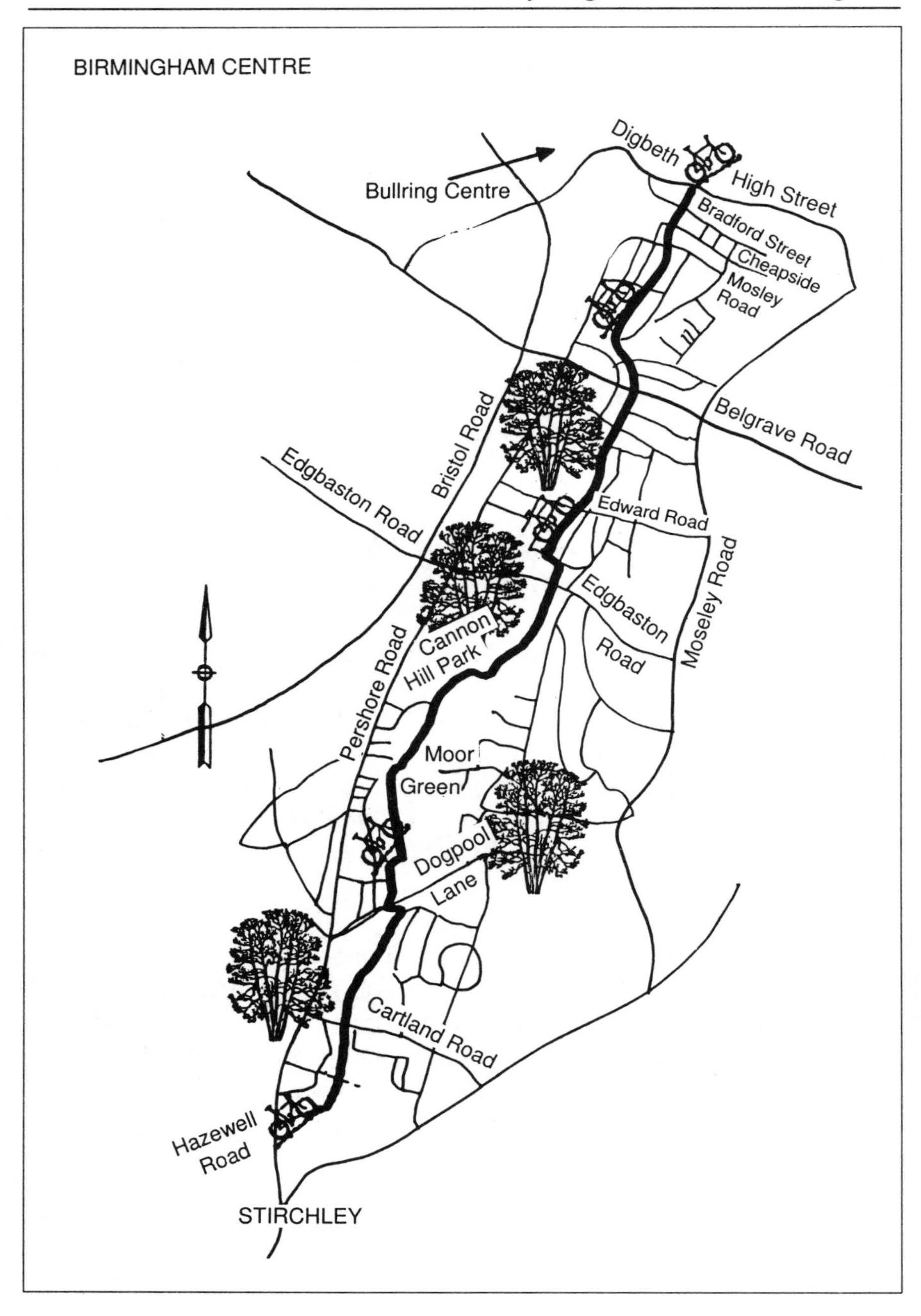
BIRMINGHAM CENTRE
Bullring Centre
Digbeth
High Street
Bradford Street
Cheapside
Mosley Road
Belgrave Road
Bristol Road
Edgbaston Road
Edward Road
Moseley Road
Edgbaston Road
Cannon Hill Park
Pershore Road
Moor Green
Dogpool Lane
Cartland Road
Hazewell Road
STIRCHLEY

A41 at Digbeth. Cannon Hill Park has a good car park and the cycle route is easily accessible from Birmingham University by crossing the Pershore Road.

The Route

Starting at the cycle path in Hazelwell Road, Stirchley, it is simply a matter of cycling until you can cycle no more. At this point you will find yourself by the A41 in Digbeth, just to the east of the Bull Ring Centre and not far from Moor Street Station. Spend some time along the route and you will see Birmingham in a very different light, even if you think you know the area well.

To start from the city centre, look out for the very clear waymarks from the Digbeth area of the city and simply follow the route in a broadly southerly direction.

Nearby

Edgbaston Cricket ground has been the venue for many test and county cricket matches. The club has an excellent youth training programme and the spectator facilities are amongst the best in England. Cannon Hill Park is one of the finest public parks in the Birmingham area.

Ride 18

Under Spaghetti Junction

A ride along the canal towing-path under Spaghetti Junction. Watch the twentieth century go by over your head while you catch a carp.

Maps: Landranger 1:50000 series. Sheet number 139

Distance: 8½ miles (13.5 km) return

Waymarked: Excellent signposting along the canal plus bridge numbers and various lock or tunnel features which make the route very easy to follow.

Gradients: Only within the lock rises

Surface: There are some narrow and possibly slippery conditions between Salford Junction and Garrison Locks. Otherwise superb cycling conditions with a mixture of smooth brick setts and a consolidated level surface.

Future Proposals: N/A

Shops and Refreshments: Good facilities around the Gas Street Basin and plenty of other opportunities from bridge exits along the route.

Special Warnings: Beware of mooring spikes, ropes and slippery edges.

Permits: A British Waterways permit is required.

This eight and a half mile return ride is an absolute delight, both in terms of cycling conditions and surrounding interest. Long lengths of the towpath are surfaced in smooth brick setts, while other parts are finished in a consolidated surface which is ideal for walkers and cyclists. Only a short length of this towing-path offers anything but ideal conditions, and the sections which are narrow and possibly slippery when wet do nothing to detract from the interest of the ride.

Amongst many other features along the route is the Birmingham Science Museum, which can be reached from the Farmer's Bridge Lock flight. This flight of locks is of special interest because of the way that the enormous buildings, both modern and old, spill out over the canal. In more than one place the whole canal is roofed in and the pounds between locks disappear into dark depths under massive concrete spans.

Under a bridge on the BCN

It is sometimes hard to tell what is new and what is old and renovated. The contrast between the canal and the outside world is akin to time travel, especially at the peak of one of Birmingham's many rush hours.

Access Points

Gas Street Basin, in the centre of Birmingham, has good car parking and the train links are excellent.

The Route

1. Leave Gas Street Basin heading towards Farmer's Bridge Junction (left as you face the water) and turn right along the Birmingham Canal, signposted to Fazeley. You will immediately start to pass the descending thirteen locks of the Farmer's Bridge flight.
2. After about half a mile you will pass the Birmingham Science Museum by lock number 10.
3. A mile further along you will arrive at Aston Junction. Join the Birmingham and Fazeley Canal and keep left to pass the de-

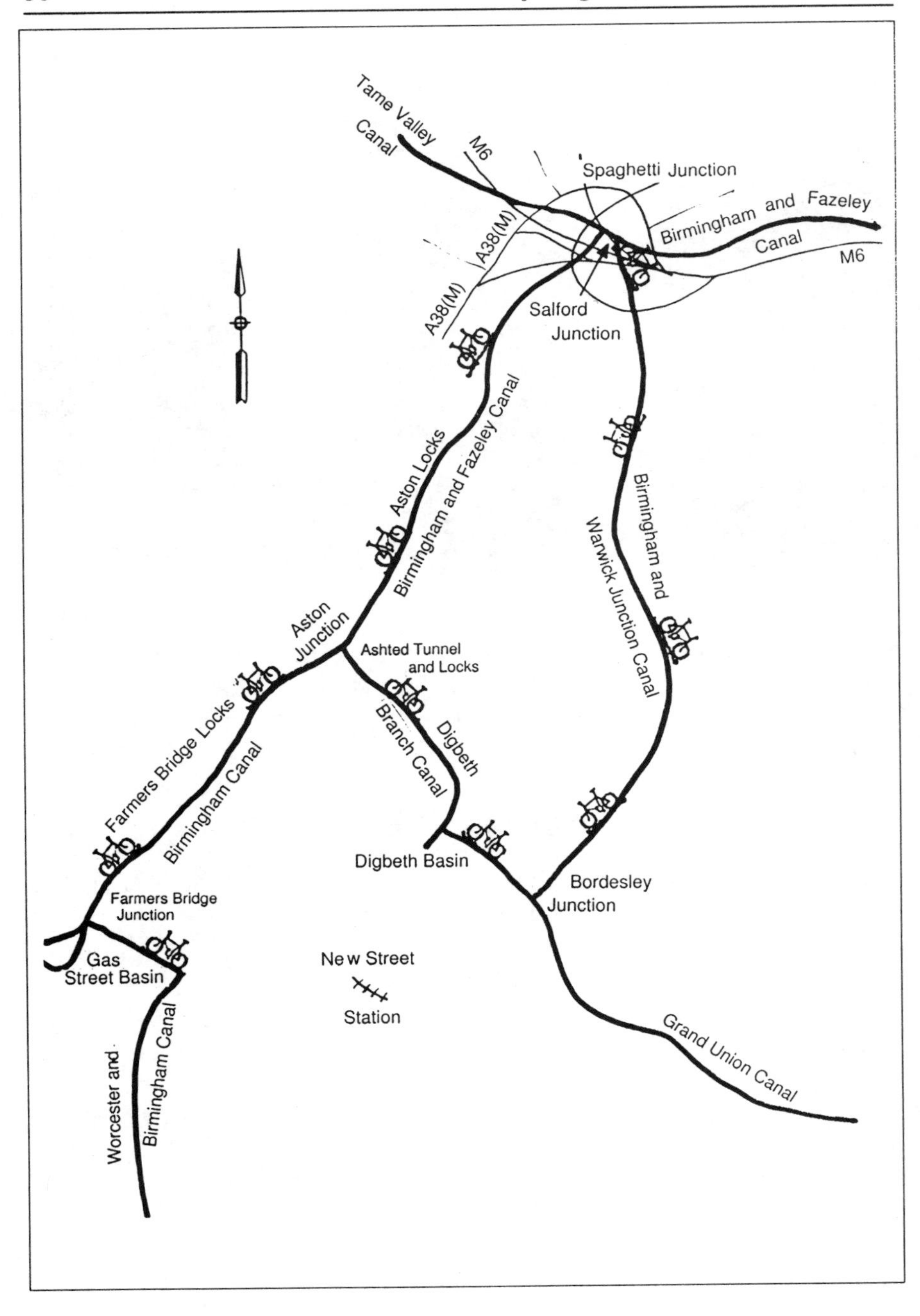
Tame Valley Canal
M6
Spaghetti Junction
Birmingham and Fazeley Canal
M6
A38(M)
A38(M)
Salford Junction
Aston Locks
Birmingham and Fazeley Canal
Birmingham and Warwick Junction Canal
Aston Junction
Ashted Tunnel and Locks
Farmers Bridge Locks
Birmingham Canal
Digbeth Branch Canal
Digbeth Basin
Bordesley Junction
Farmers Bridge Junction
Gas Street Basin
New Street Station
Worcester and Birmingham Canal
Grand Union Canal

scending eleven locks of the Aston Flight. (The towpath is on the right, signposted to Salford Junction.)

4. After about another one and a half miles, you will arrive at Salford Junction under the massive Spaghetti Junction. Turn sharp right onto the Birmingham and Warwick Junction Canal, signposted to Warwick. (The towpath is on the right. There are two right turns here, make sure you take the second.)
5. After passing the five ascending locks of the Garrison Flight, you will arrive at Bordesley Junction. Turn right along the Digbeth Branch Canal. (The towpath is on the left.)
6. Pass Digbeth Basin and cross under a massive railway crossing.
7. Very shortly after this you will need to dismount to pass through Ashted Tunnel. You then begin to pass the six ascending Ashted locks.
8. Arrive at Aston Junction and turn left to return to Farmer's Bridge Junction.
9. Just under nine miles after setting out, after retracing your outward route from Farmer's Bridge Junction, you will arrive back at Gas Street Basin.

Nearby

The short, but dark, Ashted Tunnel is situated among the six locks of the Ashted flight and opens out into a magnificently refurbished basin area at Ashted Top Lock. Any observer who knew the Ashted Tunnel area in the late 1960s would agree that here is one of the most remarkable and pleasing transformations on the BCN in recent years.

The excellent Birmingham Science Museum can be accessed from the Farmer's Bridge Flight of locks. It is well worth a visit if time allows.

The Post Office Tower can be seen for miles and is always in view from the Aston Lock flight. This route passes the very base of the tower at the Farmer's Bridge flight.

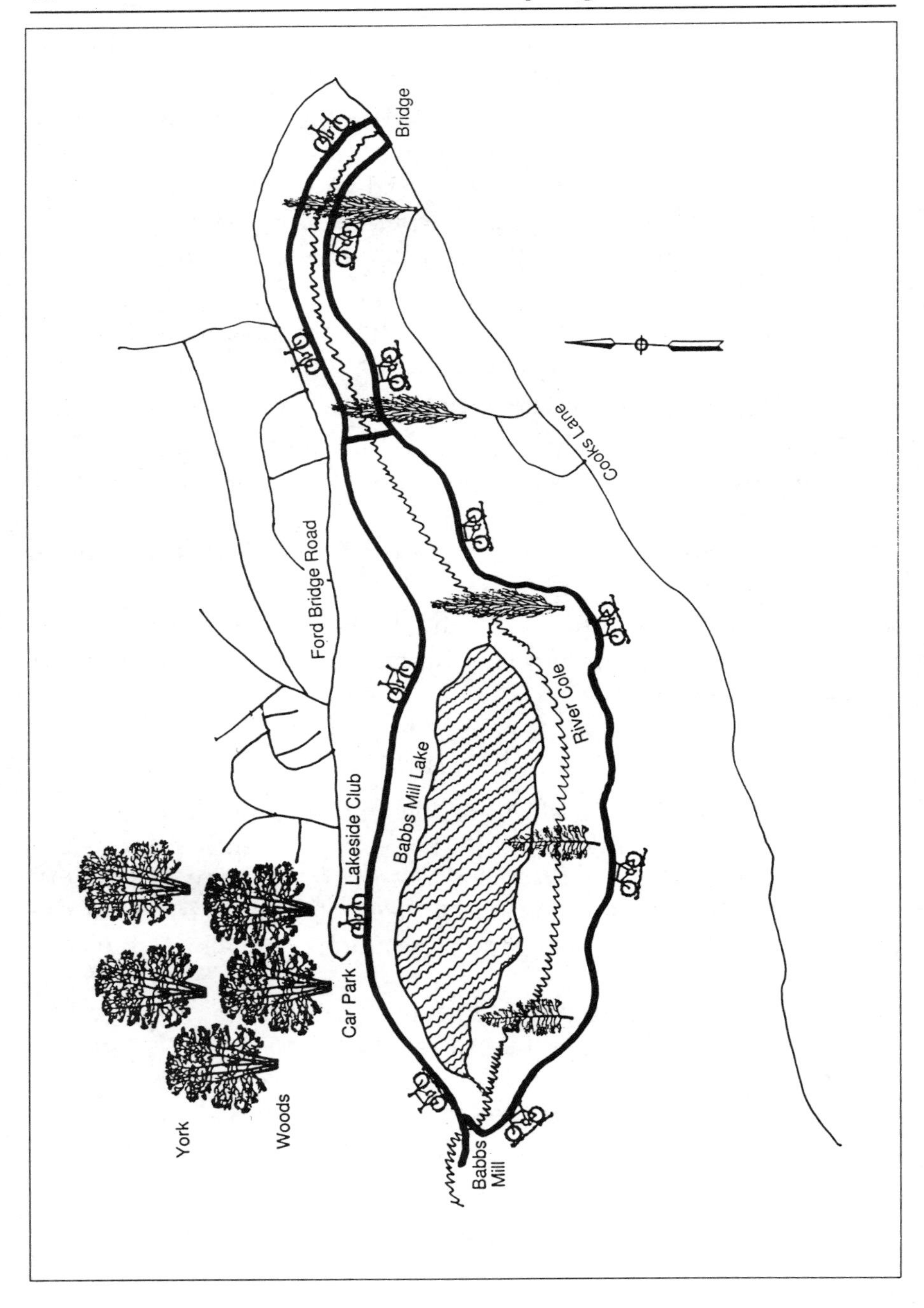
Bridge
Cooks Lane
Ford Bridge Road
River Cole
Babbs Mill Lake
Lakeside Club
Car Park
York
Woods
Babbs
Mill

Ride 19

Project Kingfisher, River Cole valley, near Chelmsley Wood

A waterside and semi-rural ride based on Project Kingfisher in the north Solihull area near Chelmsley Wood.

Maps: Landranger 1:50000 series. Sheet number 139

Distance: Total loop ride 3 miles (5 km)

Waymarked: The paths are easy to follow.

Gradients: None

Surface: Well made up, off-road cycle and walking track

Future Proposals: N/A

Shops and Refreshments: An ideal venue for a picnic and shops are never far away.

Special Warnings: N/A

Permits: N/A

This is an extremely pleasant, short waterside ride along made up, traffic-free pathways. It is ideal for a gentle fitness routine or for a short introductory family ride away from traffic. It is a delightful part of the River Cole valley and passes through meadows with wild roses, willow and alder trees, and around Babbs Lake. Centred on a convenient car park, this is a short ride and is ideal for introducing youngsters to the joys of cycling away from roads and traffic.

If you are lucky, you may see a fox peeping out of the undergrowth and keep an eye open for kestrels overhead. They may be circling over the reeds looking for voles or mice.

Access Points

Babbs Mill car park is on Ford Bridge Road, a turning off Cooks Lane which is situated off the A47, Chester Road.

The Route

1. From Babbs Mill car park, cross over the river via the metal-railed bridge then turn left through the gates to set off along the track on the south side of Babbs Lake.

2. Follow the track beyond the end of the lake for about a mile and a half up to Cooks Lane.
3. Turn left over the bridge to re-cross the river, and turn left to set off along the north side of the river to return towards Babbs Lake.
4. The track will take you across the north side of Babbs Lake and back to Babbs Mill.

Nearby

Babbs Mill is believed to have derived its name from the Babbs family who operated the mill during the 1600s. Ancient maps and records show a mill on this site as early as the 13th century, and corn was still being milled on the site in the early part of the twentieth century.

By the lake

Leisure activities around Babbs lake, which was created as a flood prevention measure, include sailing, fishing, birdwatching and walking, as well as cycling.

Ride 20

The Avoncroft Museum of Historic Buildings

Country lanes, locks and a visit to the superb open-air museum of historic buildings. Amazingly unspoilt countryside and a superb ride near to Bromsgrove and Redditch.

Maps: Landranger 1:50000 series. Sheet numbers 139 and 150

Distance: 27 miles (43.5 km) return

Waymarked: No

Gradients: Very easy. Just a few short climbs.

Surface: Tarmac country lanes

Future Proposals: N/A

Shops and Refreshments: Plenty of pubs and village shops along the way

Special Warnings: N/A

Permits: N/A

This route passes through lovely countryside just on the edge of the busy towns of Redditch and Bromsgrove. It is a moderately easy half day's ride and although it is entirely on public roads, the traffic is extremely light and therefore unlikely to spoil your cycling pleasure. There are many sections along the ride where you will have a chance to see some wonderful hedgerow flowers.

The going is generally easy, with just a few short uphill sections to stretch your legs. The ride is virtually all rural, it crosses and re-crosses the Worcester and Birmingham Canal in several places and there are plenty of good stopping places along the way including canal side pubs and relaxing little villages. If you have time, the Avoncroft Museum of Historic Buildings is well worth a visit.

Access Points

The Avoncroft Museum of Historic Buildings is situated two miles south of Bromsgrove off the A38 Bromsgrove bypass, about 400 metres from its junction with the B4091. It is well signposted from all directions and there is a good-sized visitors' car park.

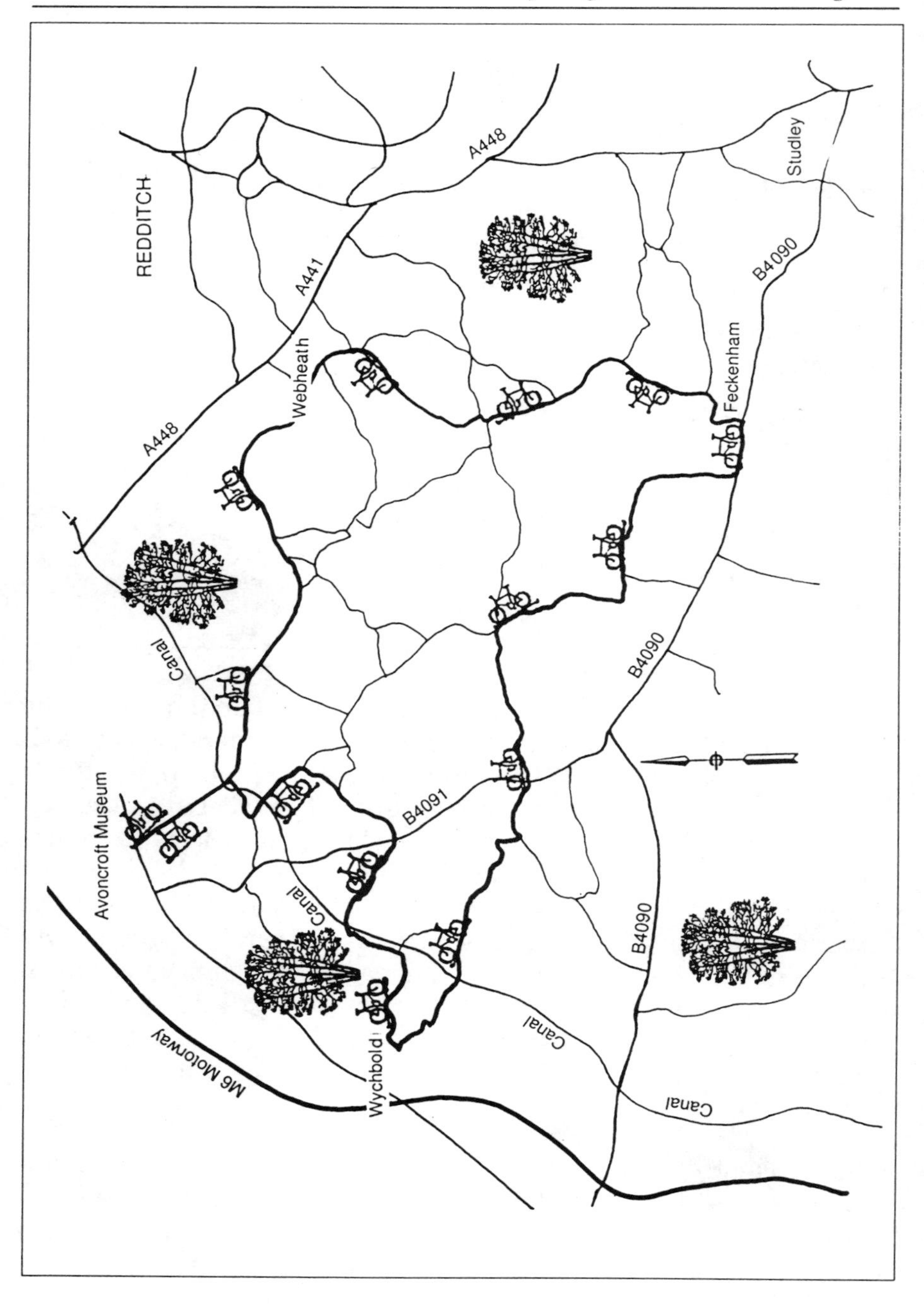
REDDITCH
A448
A441
A448
Studley
B4090
Webheath
Feckenham
Canal
B4090
B4091
Avoncroft Museum
Canal
B4090
Canal
M6 Motorway
Wychbold
Canal

The Route

1. Start at the entrance to the Avoncroft Museum of Historic Buildings.
2. Turn right out of the main car park of the Avoncroft Museum (away from the main road).
3. Following the road signposted to Stoke Pound, after about half a mile you go under a railway bridge. After a further quarter of a mile, go past The Queen's Head public house and over the Worcester and Birmingham Canal.
4. After crossing the canal take the left turn into Copyholt Lane.
5. Continue along Copyholt Lane, following the road signposted to Web Heath and Redditch.
6. After about four miles continue straight ahead, following the road signposted to Redditch (ignoring the left turn).
7. At the mini roundabout, go right, signposted to Golf Course and Feckenham. Follow the road around to the right at the first bend as it goes into Crumpfields Lane.
8. At the T-junction of Sillins Lane, turn right and then immediately left by The Book Inn public house into Ham Green Lane, signposted to Feckenham and Ham Green.
9. At the next junction turn right, signposted to Feckenham.
10. At the Swansbrook Lane and Astwood Lane T-junction, turn right towards Feckenham.
11. Pass through the very pretty Feckenham village and at the T-junction with the B4090, opposite the Lygon Arms public house, turn right into Droitwich Road, signposted to Droitwich.
12. After a short distance take the first right turn, signposted to Berrowhill and Ditchford Bank.
13. At the next junction go straight ahead (effectively right).
14. At the crossroads go left, signposted to Hanbury and Droitwich.
15. At the staggered crossroads over the B4091, go straight on (right/left) into School Road, signposted to Hanbury Hall and Droitwich.

16. Take the first right turn, towards the high ground and Hanbury Church.
17. After climbing for a short distance, take the left turn away from the church (go straight ahead to view this lovely old church).
18. After crossing the Worcester and Birmingham Canal and passing under a railway bridge, you will pass over another railway bridge and come to a T-junction. Turn right here.
19. Pass through the village of Wychbold and follow the road signposted to the Stoke Works.
20. After passing back under the railway, you see the Worcester and Birmingham Canal on your right. After following it for a while, turn right into Weston Hall Road by The Boat and Railway public house.
21. Cross the canal and follow along this road with the Stoke Works on your left-hand side.
22. At the junction with the B4091, go straight ahead at this staggered junction (right/left) into Moorgate Road, signposted to Woodgate and Lower Bentley.
23. After about a mile go left at the T-junction and after a short distance you will once again cross over the Worcester and Birmingham Canal.
24. Shortly after crossing over the canal, go right into Stoke Pound Lane.
25. Follow the road around as it crosses and then re-crosses the Worcester and Birmingham Canal by The Queen's Head public house. Continue to follow the road back to your starting point at the Avoncroft Museum.

Nearby

The Avoncroft Museum of Historic Buildings is a fine, open-air museum displaying a unique collection of old buildings which give the visitor a great insight into the way that our ancestors lived. The buildings are not necessarily grand or beautiful, but they tell their story in a way that no picture, film or text book could ever replicate.

The Avoncroft Museum

The buildings are not passive because wherever possible the museum brings them to life with demonstrations of real-life activity, carried out, often in full dress, in the authentic style of our ancestors. These displays and demonstrations cover a wide range of activity such as milling in a real, working windmill; smithing in an ancient forge using the tools, materials and techniques of a blacksmith; baking in an old range or rack-sawing timber in a reconstructed sawmill.

Ride 21

Tanworth-in-Arden

A figure-of-eight rural ride centred on the delightful village of Tanworth-in-Arden, and visiting Earlswood reservoir.

Maps: Landranger 1:50000 series. Sheet number 139

Distance: 13 miles (21 km)

Waymarked: No

Gradients: Nothing too daunting

Surface: Tarmac country lanes

Future Proposals: N/A

Shops and Refreshments: Pubs and small shops in Earlswood and Tanworth-in-Arden and pubs along the way

Special Warnings: N/A

Permits: N/A

Tanworth-in-Arden is often considered as one of the most beautiful and unspoilt little villages in the south Birmingham area. With its picturesque church, green, old pub and beautiful timbered houses, it has all of those typical English picture postcard qualities. You may be lucky on a summer's evening to arrive in the village and find morris dancers performing on the green, it is that sort of place.

Figuratively, the ride is a figure of eight shape centred on Tanworth-in-Arden. It passes along beautiful little lanes, exploring the surrounding area, and eventually reaches the causeway across Earlswood Reservoir from where it returns to Tanworth-in-Arden.

Access Points

The route is described from the Tanworth-in-Arden village centre. To get to Tanworth-in-Arden, take the B4101 west away from the A34(T) at Hockley Heath.

The Route

1. From the centre of Tanworth-in-Arden, with your back to the pub and with the church away to your left, turn right along the village street and take the left turn down Bates Lane.
2. At the crossroad junction turn left into Forde Hall Lane.
3. After about one and half miles, turn left into Gentleman's Lane, signposted to Tanworth-in-Arden.
4. At the T-junction at the end of Gentleman's Lane, turn left into Ramshill Lane.
5. Follow Ramshill Lane under the railway and shortly after this turn left at the T-junction signposted to Tanworth-in-Arden.
6. Follow this road through the village of Danzey Green, over the railway and past Danzey Green Station back to Tanworth-in-Arden village centre.
7. Go through the village once again, this time ignoring the left turn along Bates Lane and following the road signposted to Hockley Heath.
8. At the junction with the B4101 go right, signposted to Hockley Heath, and after a very short distance turn left into Poolhead Road, signposted to Forshaw Heath.
9. After crossing the motorway go right, signposted to Terry's Green, cross the railway and continue straight ahead onto the causeway of Earlswood Lakes. Take the right fork on the causeway.
10. At the crossroads by The Reservoir public house in Earlswood, take the road signposted to Solihull, and after a very short distance turn left into Leafy Lane, signposted to Hockley Heath.
11. After a short distance turn left, signposted to Solihull.
12. Turn right by The Bull's Head public house into Lime Kiln Lane.
13. At the T-junction, with the canal on your left-hand side and a pub straight ahead, turn right into Warings Green Road.

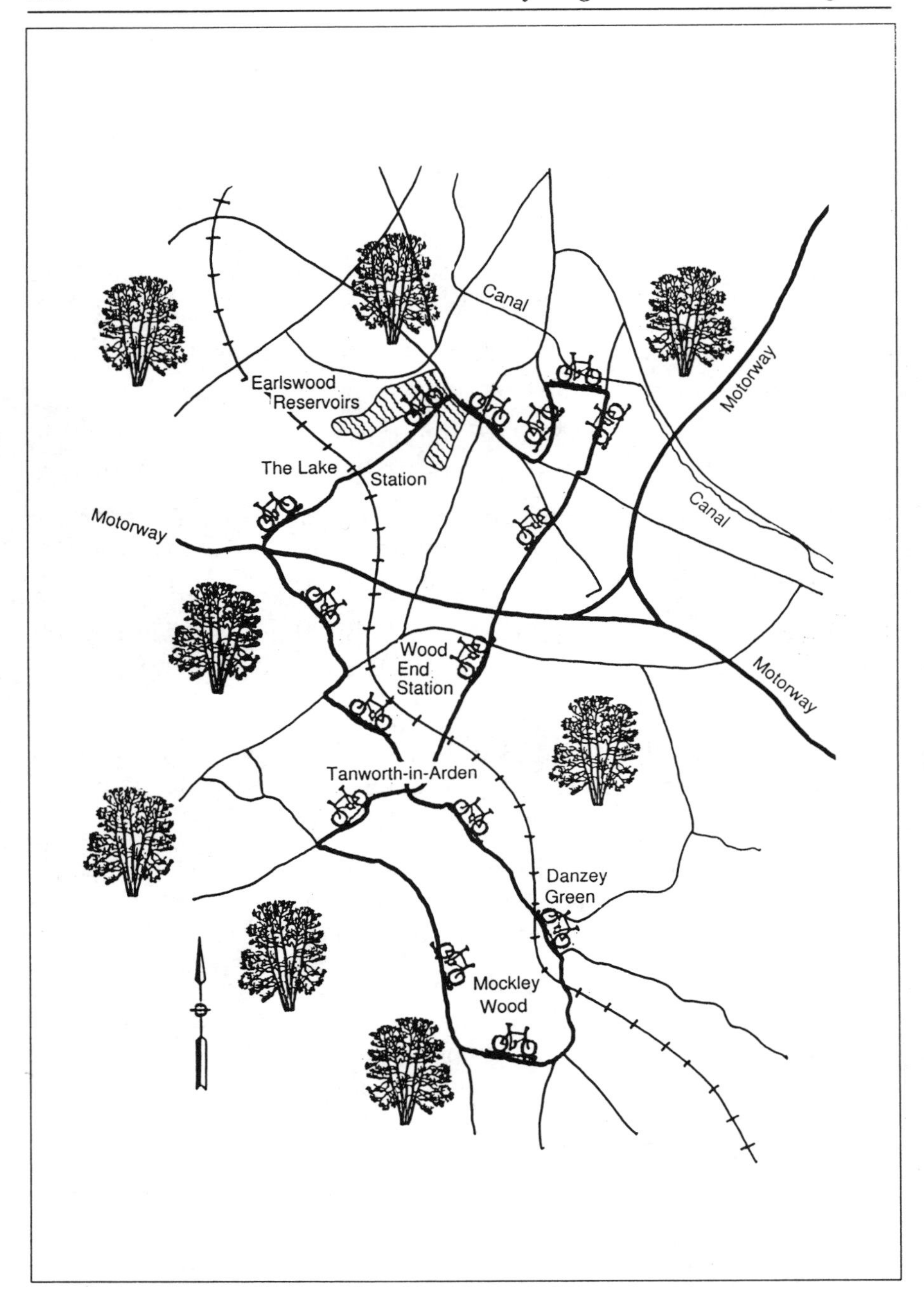
Canal
Motorway
Earlswood
Reservoirs
The Lake
Station
Motorway
Canal
Wood
End
Station
Motorway
Tanworth-in-Arden
Danzey
Green
Mockley
Wood

14. Go straight ahead at the crossroads and after passing over the motorway, continue to go straight on at the next crossroads junction with the B4101.
15. Follow 'the signs to Tanworth-in-Arden village centre.

Nearby

Earlswood Reservoir is a well-known reservoir and beauty spot consisting of three inter-linked lakes which are known as Windmill Pool, Engine Pool and Terry's Pool. Their purpose is to feed water to the summit level of the Stratford-upon-Avon Canal. This is done by means of an insignificant-looking feeder channel which meets the canal near Bridge 16, about half a mile to the north of the reservoir.

The M42 was built during the 1980s to form the last side of the motorway triangle which surrounds Birmingham.

Some steep hills south of Tanworth, but north is a fairly level ride.

Ride 22

Lapworth and surrounding villages

Begins at the junction of The Grand Union and Stratford-upon-Avon Canals. A very pretty, rural ride taking in Hay Wood and an unusual number of country and canal side pubs.

Maps: Landranger 1:50000 series. Sheet number 139

Distance: 15 miles (24 km)

Waymarked: No

Gradients: A few very gentle slopes.

Surface: Mainly tarmac country lanes but some muddy tracks and canal towpath plus the possibility of exploring Hay Wood. An attractive proposition for a mountain bike but a good tourer will also suffice.

Future Proposals: N/A

Shops and Refreshments: Numerous canal side pubs and a few village shops

Special Warnings: N/A

Permits: A British Waterways permit is required. At times cycling is prohibited on this towpath but the situation is under regular review.

This ride weaves its way around a maze of lovely, quiet country lanes, roughly centred on Lapworth. The countryside is magnificent and the ride is made all the more interesting by the fact that it crosses the canals of the area on no less than six occasions, as well as routing alongside both the Stratford-upon-Avon Canal and the Grand Union Canal for short stretches.

If you become bored with your bicycle, there is an unusually rich choice of diversion along this route. Try one of the many canal side pubs along the way or take a gentle stroll in Hay Wood. Baddesley Clinton and Packwood House are both great old houses with plenty of interest, and they are both well worth a visit. If you want a gentle weekend cycle ride in the country, this would be an ideal choice.

Access Points

To find the British Waterways Kingswood canal yard at Lapworth

The junction of two canals

and the junction of the Stratford-upon-Avon and the Grand Union Canals, take the B4439 either south east from Hockley Heath or north west from Hatton near Warwick. Lapworth station is just a few hundred metres away from the B4439.

The Route

1. Start at the exit to the British Waterways Kingswood canal yard at Lapworth, by the junction of the Stratford-upon-Avon and the Grand Union Canals.
2. Turn left out of the yard (away from the main road) and follow the lane as it leads into a farm track.
3. Past the farmyard, continue to follow the track as it becomes narrower and surrounded by more trees and hedging.
4. After about a quarter of a mile, take the left-hand fork in the track and after a very short distance you will come out on the Stratford-upon-Avon Canal by lock 25 and bridge 39.
5. Cross over bridge 39 and continue past the lock cottage and onto a tarmac lane (Dick's Lane).

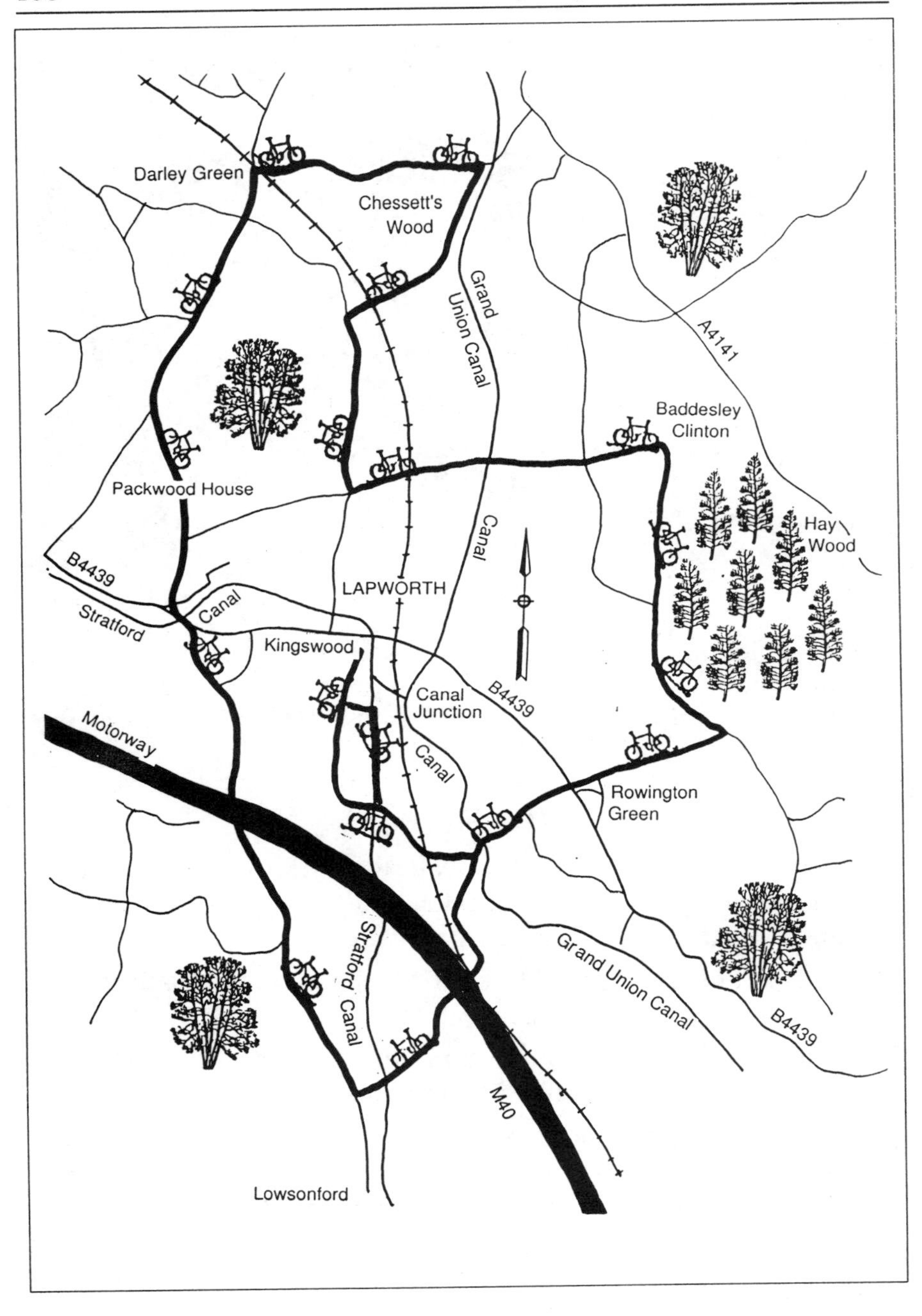
Darley Green
Chessett's Wood
Grand Union Canal
A4141
Baddesley Clinton
Packwood House
Hay Wood
Canal
B4439
Canal
LAPWORTH
Stratford
Kingswood
Canal Junction
B4439
Motorway
Canal
Rowington Green
Stratford Canal
Grand Union Canal
B4439
M40
Lowsonford

6. Follow Dick's Lane as it passes under a railway bridge and you will come out by the Grand Union Canal and the Tom-O-the-Wood public house.
7. Go right here, away from the Tom-O-the-Wood public house and the canal bridge. After about half a mile you will pass over the M40 and shortly beyond you will come into the village of Lowsensford.
8. Cross the Stratford-upon-Avon Canal here at bridge 40 and then immediately turn right, signposted to Lapworth and Hockley Heath. (If you turn left here it is only a very short distance down to the Fleur-de-Lys Public House.)
9. After a short distance you will once again cross the M40. Continue along this road to the junction with the B4439.
10. Turn left along the B4439 (if you go right here you will shortly come to The Boot public House).
11. After a very short distance and after crossing the Grand Union Canal, go right, signposted to Chadwick End, Packwood House and Baddesley Clinton.
12. Follow the road signposted to Packwood House and then follow through the grounds of the house.
13. After passing Packwood House, you will shortly arrive at a crossroads. Go straight on to Darley Green.
14. In Darley Green, by the green, turn right.
15. Just before the Grand Union Canal, turn right to follow Baker's Lane alongside the canal (with the water on your left).
16. At the T-junction turn left, signposted to Lapworth and Hockley Heath.
17. At the crossroads by The Punch Bowl public house, turn left, signposted to Lapworth Station, Chadwick End and Baddesley Clinton.
18. Cross the Grand Union Canal once again, and after about a mile take the right turn signposted to Mousley End and Hay Wood.
19. Pass Hay Wood on your left. (You will catch glimpses of Baddesley Clinton on your right.) After passing Hay Wood, take the

right turn at the grassy triangle, signposted to Rowington and Lapworth.

20. At the crossroads with the B4439 go straight ahead, signposted to Lowsensford.
21. After passing the Tom-O-the-Wood public house and crossing over the Grand Union Canal, turn right along Dick's Lane to retrace the outbound route.
22. As an alternative to the track, and subject to British Waterways current cycling notices, you may wish to copy the example of many local cyclists and return to the Lapworth maintenance road via the Stratford-upon-Avon Canal towing-path. To do this turn right by bridge 39 to pass lock 25 on your left.

Nearby

Packwood House is notable for its array of clipped yew hedging which purports to be a representation of the Sermon on the Mount. The timber-framed house, with its warm, red brick insets and mullioned windows, dates back to the 16th century, but it was substantially extended in the 17th century by John Featherstone. It is open on summer afternoons and amongst its displays are tapestry, needlework and furniture.

Ride 23

Warwick Castle to Leamington Spa.

A glorious rural route from Warwick and its medieval castle to Regency Leamington Spa.

Maps: Landranger 1:50000 series. Sheet numbers: mainly 151 but also 139 and 140.

Distance: 22 miles (35.5 km) return

Waymarked: No

Gradients: Some slight climbs

Surface: Tarmac country lanes

Future Proposals: N/A

Shops and Refreshments: Plenty of shops, pubs and restaurants along the way

Special Warnings: A couple of short stretches where you will unavoidably need to use main roads. In most cases there are footpaths.

Permits: N/A unless you return to Warwick via the Grand Union Canal towing-path from Hatton. The towpath regulations may require you to carry a permit and push your bicycle at some stages. Cycling sometimes prohibited on this towing-path.

This lovely, mainly rural ride starts and ends at the historic town of Warwick which boasts one of England's finest castles. Starting in St Nicholas Park, the first encounter you will have with Warwick Castle is the superb view, up the Avon towards the eastern walls. Shortly after setting off you are quite likely to encounter peacocks from the glorious castle grounds in Castle Lane.

The ride leaves Warwick by the racecourse and heads out into the pleasant countryside to the east. After exploring the villages of Norton Lindsey, Shrewley and Haseley, the route heads around the north of Warwick and passes through the villages of Leek Wootton and Hill Wootton before skirting the edge of Leamington Spa and returning to Warwick via Old Milverton.

This is a very pleasant and undemanding half day's ride which succeeds in avoiding busy roads except for one half-mile section just north of Leamington Spa. There are numerous stopping off points, pubs and shops along the route and there are plenty of interesting diversions such as the craft centre just outside Hatton.

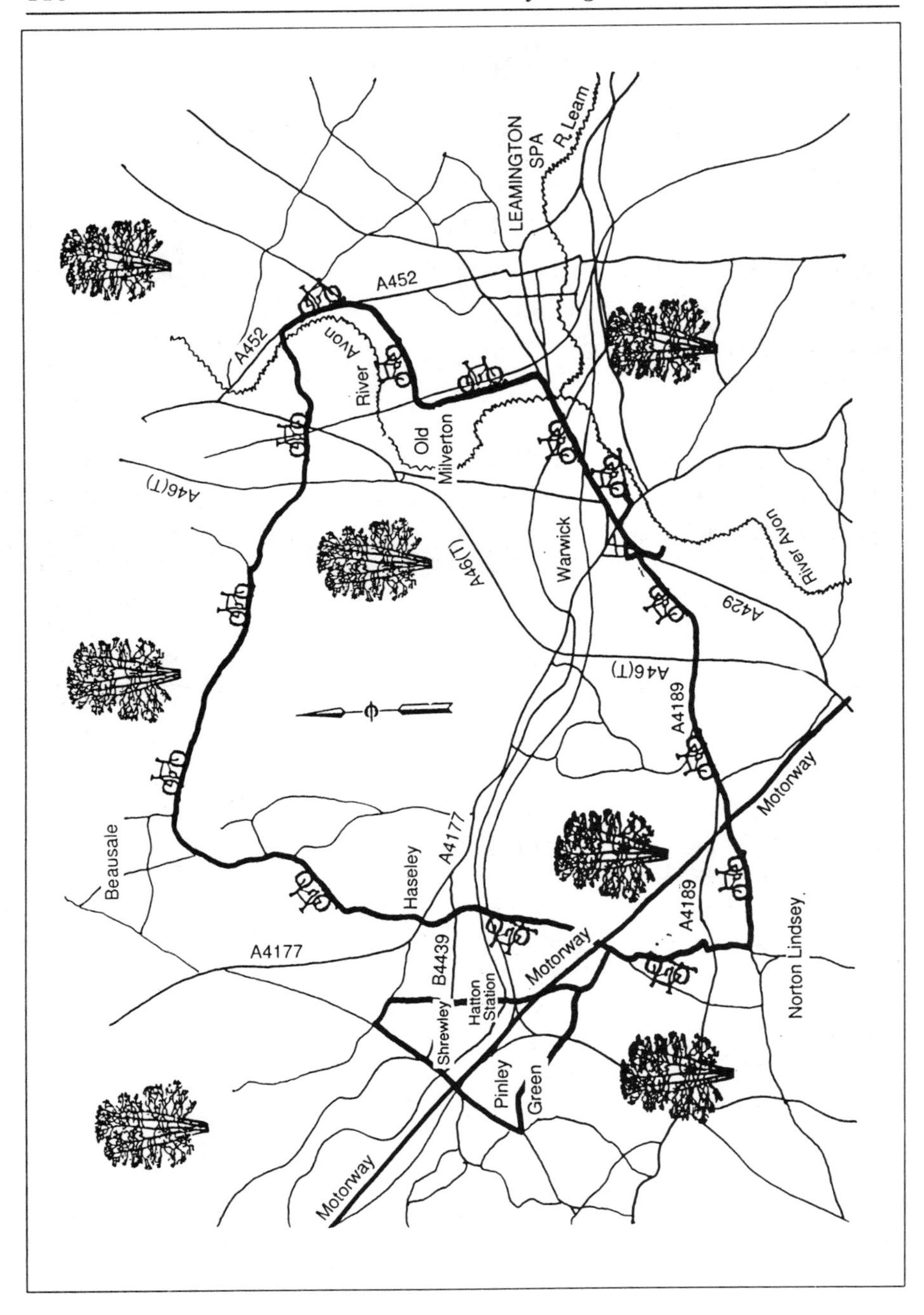
LEAMINGTON SPA
R.Leam
A452
A452
River Avon
Old Milverton
A46(T)
A46(T)
Warwick
River Avon
A429
A46(T)
A4189
Motorway
A4189
Norton Lindsey
Beausale
Haseley
A4177
A4177
B4439
Hatton Station
Motorway
Shrewley
Pinley Green
Motorway

Hasely Church

Access Points

St Nicholas Park is situated to the east of central Warwick. The car park is situated off the A41, just before the River Avon bridge.

The Route

1. From the car park of St Nicholas Park in Warwick, head towards the main road with the castle in view ahead of you.
2. Turn right out of the car park, signposted to Town Centre and Warwick Castle. Continue straight ahead at the traffic island by the castle gate and then, after a very short distance, turn left into Castle Lane.
3. After following along Castle Lane with the castle walls on your left (you may see some peacocks), turn right into Back Lane.
4. At the end of Back Lane turn right and then immediately left into Swan Street.
5. Turn right into the main square and then left at the far end, signposted to Car Parks and Through Traffic. Turn left at the traffic lights.

6. After a very short distance, turn right into Linen Street and then left through the bollards at the bottom onto the racecourse perimeter road.
7. At the exit to the racecourse, turn right along the A4189 and follow this road for about two miles. The route goes out of Warwick, over the bypass and to the left-hand junction signposted to Norton Lindsey. Then go immediately right, also signposted to Norton Lindsey.
8. After crossing the motorway, turn right at the crossroads into Brittons Lane, signposted to Hatton.
9. At the staggered crossroads with the A4189, go straight on (right and immediately left) into the single track lane.
10. At the T-junction turn right, signposted to Hatton, and after a very short distance, just before the motorway bridge, turn left, signposted to Hatton Station.
11. Follow this road and signposts to Pinley (ignoring the right turn to Hatton Station).
12. At Pinley Green turn right, signposted to Shrewley. Follow this road over the motorway and railway, through the built-up area of Shrewley Common to the crossroads of the B4439. Go straight ahead at these crossroads.
13. After about a quarter of a mile, take the right turn signposted to Little Shrewley into Stoney Lane.
14. After a very short distance go right, signposted to Little Shrewley and Hatton Station, into Mill Lane. At the bottom of Mill Lane go straight ahead into Station Road, crossing the B4439.
15. Follow Station Road over the canal and railway and over the motorway to a T-junction. Go left here, signposted to Haseley. (You will notice that you have already cycled over this next short stretch in the opposite direction.)
16. At the T-junction go left, signposted to Hatton and Haseley, and cross over the motorway. Follow the road back over the railway and canal to another crossroads of the B4439. Go straight over at the crossroads, signposted to Hatton Green.

17. At the next crossroads with the A41, go straight ahead, signposted to Haseley. Follow the signposts to Beausale.
18. At the T-junction go left to follow the road signposted to Beausale.
19. At the edge of Beausale follow the road signposted to Kenilworth.
20. Follow this road for a while and then take the right turn signposted to Leek Wootton.
21. In the village of Leek Wootton, turn right by The Anchor public house and then immediately left into Hill Wootton Road, signposted to Hill Wootton.
22. Pass under the bypass and shortly after you will come to the crossroads with the B4115 (with a railway bridge flying diagonally over the junction). Go straight on here, signposted to Hill Wootton.
23. Go through Hill Wootton village and shortly afterwards you will come to the T-junction with the main A452, Kenilworth to Leamington road. Turn right along this road. Take care along this stretch as there is more traffic and some vehicles tend to move along quite quickly. There is a footpath for most of this stretch, initially on the right-hand side and later on the left-hand side. If you have children in your party, you may prefer to use this path for the half mile to the road island where you will make the next turn.
24. After a fairly short distance along this busy road, turn right at the road island, signposted to Old Milverton.
25. After following this road for a while you will come to a T-junction with the Rugby road, on the edge of the built-up area of Leamington Spa.
26. Turn right here and then right again at the lights to follow the road over the river and canal into Warwick.
27. Continue to follow this road (Emscote Road and Coten End). Eventually you will come out at the small island by the east gate of Warwick Castle. Turn left here to return to the starting point.

Nearby

Warwick Castle is unusual because it is one of the few medieval castles used as a residence. The castle was built in the 14th century on the site of the Norman castle which William the Conqueror gave to Henry de Newburgh, along with the title Earl of Warwick. The castle remained the seat of the Earls of Warwick for nearly 1000 years. One of the castle's most notable fortifications, Caesar's Tower, was completed in 1356 and almost immediately used to house French prisoners of war from the battle of Poiters.

The tour around the castle is full of fascination and includes every aspect of the castle, ranging from the horror of the medieval dungeons and the armoury to the splendour of the state apartments overlooking the River Avon.

Warwick was virtually destroyed by fire in 1694, but a few buildings did survive. One of the most interesting is the Lord Leycester Hospital which is a group of buildings dating back to the 12th century. Later additions were made over the years up to the 16th century. Originally, the buildings found uses as a guildhall, a grammar school and a council chambers, but in 1571 Robert Dudley, Earl of Leicester, founded a hospital on the site for those wounded in the service of the Queen and her successors. The accommodation provided for twelve men and it is still in use to this day.

Ride 24

Warwick University and Kenilworth Castle

A circular route through lanes past Crackley Woods to Kenilworth Castle and back to the University campus.

Maps: Landranger 1:50000 series. Sheet number 140

Distance: 12 miles (19.5 km)

Waymarked: No

Gradients: A few fairly undemanding slopes

Surface: Tarmac country lanes

Future Proposals: N/A

Shops and Refreshments: Numerous facilities in and around Kenilworth

Special Warnings: N/A

Permits: N/A

This short, circular route starts and ends at the University of Warwick which, despite its name, is situated nowhere near Warwick, but on the outskirts of Coventry. The route goes through lanes past Crackley Woods to the picturesque little country town of Kenilworth. In Kenilworth you will have a chance to explore the ancient ruins of the castle.

There are other marvellous old buildings in Kenilworth, including many excellent examples of genuine Tudor and Georgian architecture. Some of the most impressive buildings are the cottages behind the green opposite the castle.

If the weather is on the blustery side, this is normally a sheltered ride. If the weather is warm, there is plenty of shade cover.

Access Points

The University of Warwick is situated on the southern edge of Coventry – take the A429 from Coventry city centre towards Kenilworth.

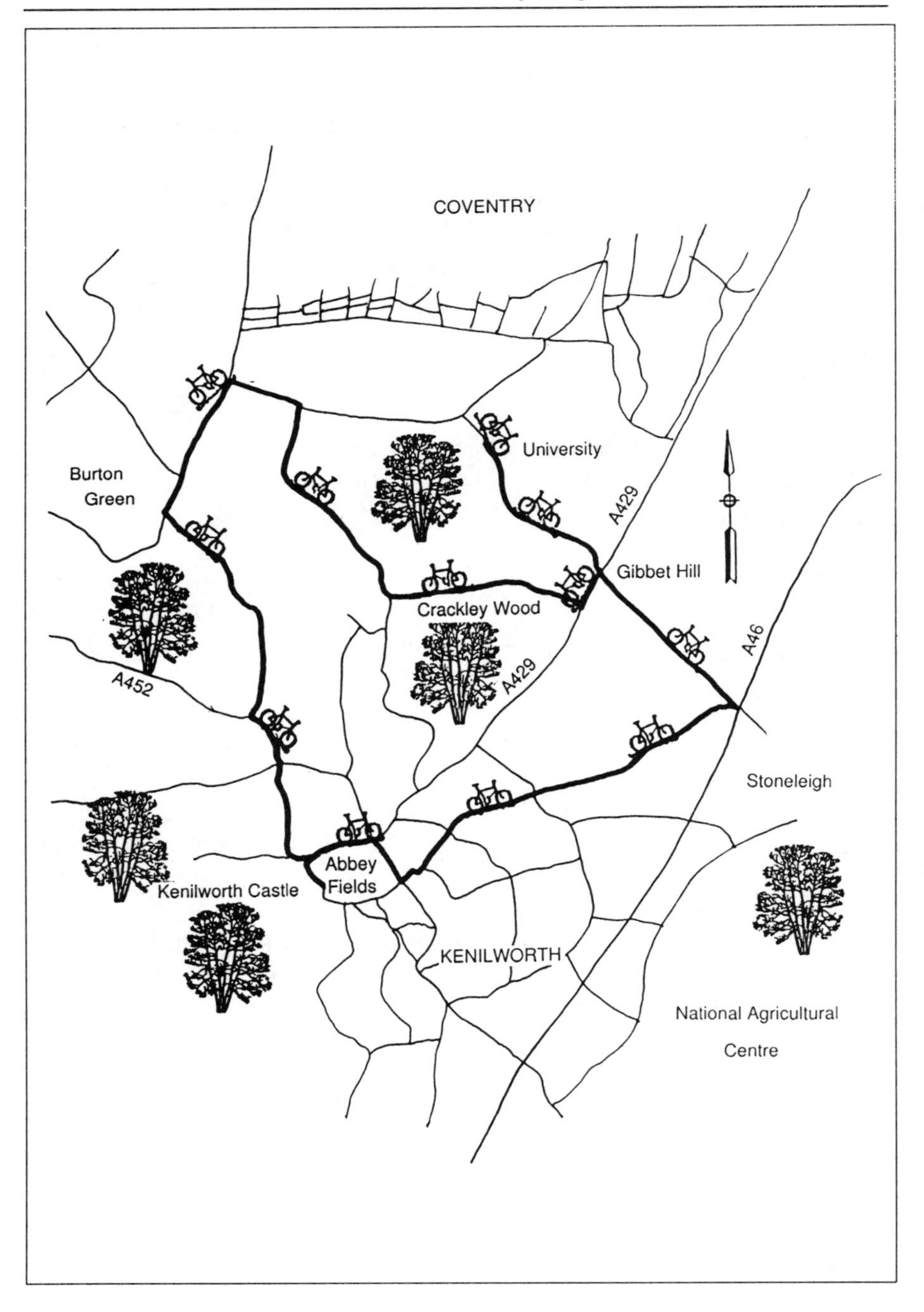

COVENTRY
University
Burton
Green
A429
Gibbet Hill
Crackley Wood
A46
A429
A452
Stoneleigh
Abbey
Fields
Kenilworth Castle
KENILWORTH
National Agricultural
Centre

The Route

1. Turn left out of the University via the main concourse and follow Gibbet Hill Road towards Kenilworth Road.
2. After about a mile, at the junction with Gibbet Hill Road and Kenilworth Road, turn right along Kenilworth Road using the footpath rather than crossing into the busy road. (Cyclists tend to use the very wide footpath on the right-hand side of the road at this point.)
3. After about a third of a mile, take the right turn into Cryfield Grange Road.
4. Follow this road for just over a mile, and when it comes to a T-junction by a grassy triangle turn right.
5. After about another mile, at the next T-junction, turn left onto the more major road (Westwood Heath Road) on the edge of the built-up area.
6. After about half a mile, turn left off Westwood Heath Road into Cromwell Lane and almost immediately you will come into the village of Burton Green.
7. Carry on through the village, cross the railway and then just as you are leaving the village, go left into Red Lane.
8. Red Lane will lead to the edge of Kenilworth. Upon reaching the T-junction, turn left and follow the well-signposted road (Clinton Lane) to Kenilworth Castle. Turn right into the castle area.
9. After exploring the castle, turn left out of the car park entrance. After a very short distance, turn right along Castle Hill.
10. At the end of Castle Hill, at traffic lights, turn right into Bridge Street.
11. After passing Abbey Fields on your right, turn left, signposted to Stoneleigh, into Upper Rosemary Hill.
12. Follow this road (it has several changes of name) out of Kenilworth.
13. At the small traffic island, go left into Stoneleigh Road and follow this road back to Kenilworth Road.
14. Go straight over Kenilworth Road into Gibbet Hill Road and follow your outbound track back to the university.

Kenilworth Castle

Nearby

As a result of Cromwell's intervention in the Civil War, Kenilworth Castle is now little more than scattered ruins with a few major structural walls and floors still in-situ. It is generally considered to be the grandest fortress ruin in England. There has been a castle on the site since 1112 AD when a substantial wooden fortress was built by Geoffrey de Clinton. The earliest building on the site is a keep that dates back to 1162. The castle enjoyed greater prominence after 1563 when Queen Elizabeth gave the castle to Robert Dudley, Earl of Leicester. Queen Elizabeth was a regular visitor to Kenilworth.

Stoneleigh is the home of the national agricultural showground and centre, the long term venue for the annual Royal Show. At the time when the show is on, the local roads can become blocked with queues of traffic, although this will not cause you any problems on your bicycle.

Ride 25

The Coventry Canal

A fascinating towing-path ride from Coventry's charming canal basins, and a chance to explore the city centre.

Maps: Landranger 1:50000 series. Sheet number 140

Distance: 8¼ miles (13.25 km) each way

Waymarked: Plenty of bridge numbers and mileposts

Gradients: None

Surface: Canal towpath – straightforward cycling conditions with the occasional slippery and narrow patch

Future Proposals: British Waterways has a policy of constant maintenance and improvement.

Shops and Refreshments: Plenty of stopping off places reached from the numerous bridges

Special Warnings: Some sections of this towing-path can be particularly slippery when wet. Watch out for mooring spikes and ropes. Do not try to cycle through the tunnel, get off and push.

Permits: British Waterways permit required.

From the canal basin in Coventry city centre, the Coventry Canal heads north. Five and a half miles from the basin it connects with the Oxford Canal at Hawkesbury Junction and then, eight and a quarter miles from the basin, it connects with the Ashby Canal at Marston Junction. Beyond Marston Junction the Coventry Canal continues north to the Trent and Mersey Canal. This ride looks at the Coventry Canal from the city basin up to Marston Junction and back, a total return trip of sixteen and a half miles. Nearly all of this way the canal is running through densely built-up areas, and the canal is often hemmed in by the backs of buildings. Between Hawkesbury Junction and Marston Junction, the canal passes through sheltered cuttings and across a wide dilapidated landscape.

Despite the fact that this entire section is in built-up areas, the surroundings on the towing-path are most pleasant and interesting.

The cycling conditions are good for urban canals but the towing-path is sometimes narrow and muddy, although always passable with care. Even allowing for the fact that you will need to slow down occasionally and generally not hurry, a reasonable average speed can be maintained for this lovely return tour.

There are some excellent and friendly canal side pubs, and leaving the towpath at virtually any bridge will usually lead to some refreshment – a pub, a garage or a corner shop.

Access Points

The Canal Basin is well signposted from Coventry Inner ring road. It is not far from the main railway station and within very easy reach of the bus station.

The Route

1. On leaving the canal basin you will need to cross over the first bridge (Draper's Field Bridge) in order to continue along the towing-path with the water on your left-hand side.
2. You will pass under several bridges before arriving at the M6 after about four miles, just after bridge number 10. After passing under the motorway, you will soon come to Hawkesbury Junction, which is five and a half miles from the city basin.
3. Continue two and three quarter miles north from Hawkesbury Junction to Marston Junction.
4. Return the way you came.

Nearby

There are many attractions in Coventry. The Herbert Art Gallery and Museum houses works by Turner, Lowry and Constable, as well as the Sutherland sketches for the Coventry Cathedral Tapestry. The remarkable ruins of the Cathedral Church of St Michael are situated close to the modern Cathedral which was designed by Sir Basil Spence and completed in 1962. The Museum of Transport houses the largest display of British-made transport in the world.

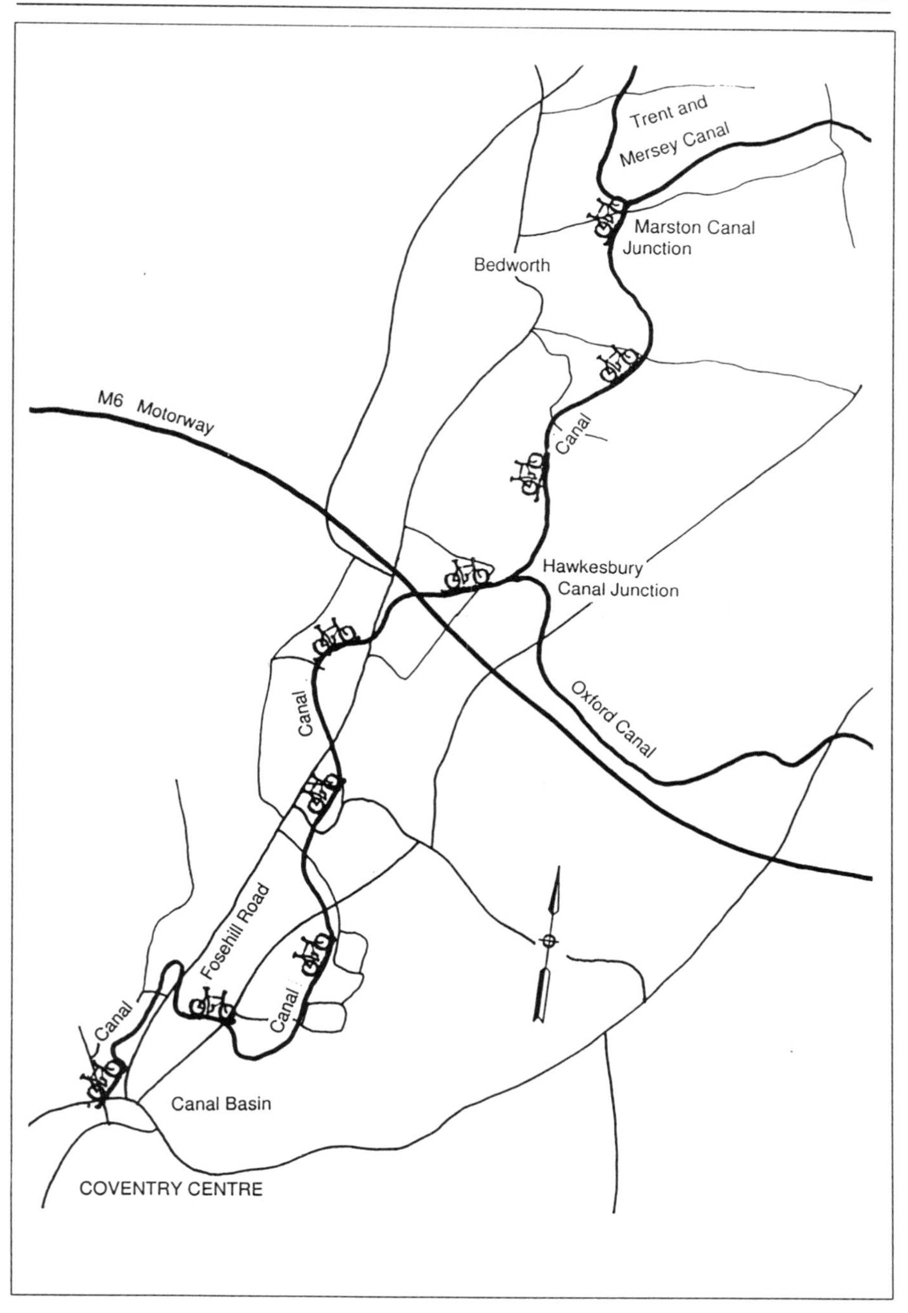
Trent and
Mersey Canal
Marston Canal
Junction
Bedworth
M6 Motorway
Canal
Hawkesbury
Canal Junction
Oxford Canal
Canal
Fosehill Road
Canal
Canal
Canal Basin
COVENTRY CENTRE

Ride 26

Stratford-upon-Avon

A Shakespearean tour from Stratford-upon-Avon. Beautiful back lanes and villages plus various Shakespearean properties.

Maps: Landranger 1:50000 series. Sheet number 151

Distance: 25½ miles (41 km) return

Waymarked: No

Gradients: One or two fairly easy climbs

Surface: Tarmac country lanes and B-roads

Future Proposals: N/A

Shops and Refreshments: Plenty of shops and pubs in villages along the route

Special Warnings: N/A

Permits: N/A

This is a tour of the countryside around the traditional Shakespearean region. It takes you from the popular Shakespearean sites in the centre of Stratford-upon-Avon out into the surrounding villages and to some of the famous tourist attractions which are normally part of the main itinerary of Shakespearean tours. Along this route are Shottery, Wilmcote, Aston Cantlow, Snitterfield, Hampton Lucy, Charlecote Deer Park and Loxley village. Virtually the whole route is via country lanes with low traffic densities. This is, therefore, a relaxing, easy ride along tarmac minor roads with some delightful views of the Avon and the surrounding rolling countryside.

After setting out from Stratford-upon-Avon, you will very soon arrive at Shottery. Even if you do not go into Anne Hathaway's house (Shakespeare's wife), you will enjoy the sight of this lovely old English scene of the cottage and the traditional English garden. Your next major feature will be found at Wilmcote with Mary Arden's cottage, home of Shakespeare's mother. After exploring more villages, you will pass through Charlecote Deer Park. It was here that Shakespeare was purported to have been caught poaching, an event that is supposed to have sparked off his sudden departure to London where he became an actor at the Globe Theatre. You will then return

Mary Arden's house

to Stratford-upon-Avon through Loxley and along the Tiddington Road, which backs onto a lovely stretch of the River Avon.

Access Points

There are plenty of well-marked car parks in Stratford-upon-Avon and the train station is only a very short ride away from the town centre. This ride is described from the Royal Shakespeare Theatre in Waterside which is clearly signed from all over Stratford-upon-Avon.

The Route

1. From the Royal Shakespeare Theatre in Waterside, in the central area of Stratford-upon-Avon, head south, away from the bridge and keeping the river and the gardens on your left.
2. At the T-junction, turn right and after a short distance go left into College Street, and then right into College Lane.
3. College Lane becomes Sanctus Street and then Sanctus Road. Follow it over the modern hump-back bridge and at the end of the road, by The Salmon Tail public house, turn sharp right onto the A4390.

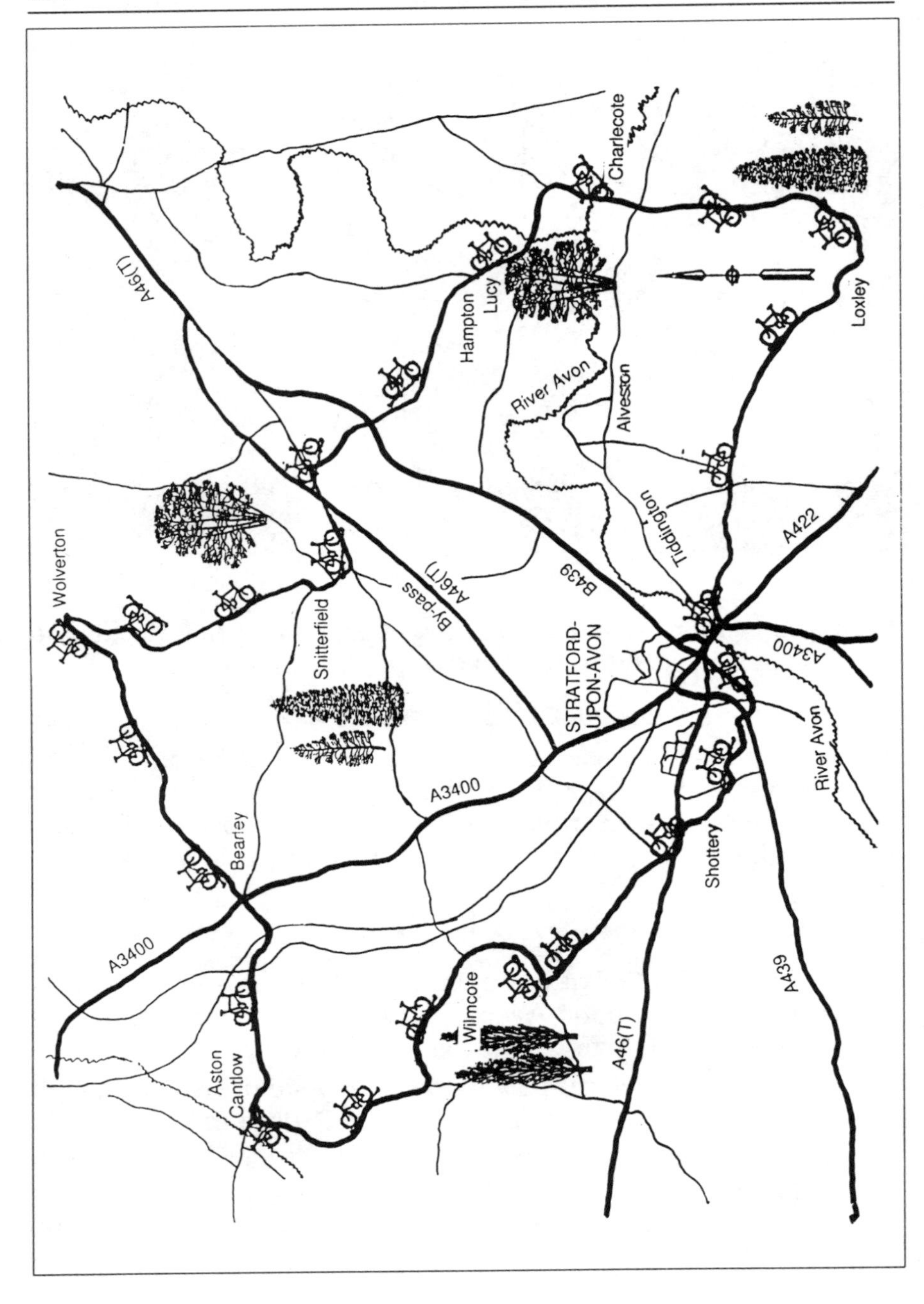
Charlecote
Hampton Lucy
Loxley
A46(T)
River Avon
Alveston
Tiddington
A422
B439
A46(T) By-pass
Wolverton
Snitterfield
STRATFORD-UPON-AVON
A3400
A3400
River Avon
Bearley
Shottery
A3400
Wilmcote
A46(T)
A439
Aston Cantlow

4. At the small traffic island go left, signposted to Shottery and Anne Hathaway's Cottage. Continue into Shottery, following the signposts to Anne Hathaway's Cottage.
5. After passing Anne Hathaway's cottage, continue straight on to the T-junction with South Green Drive. Turn right, signposted to Main Road.
6. A short distance along South Green Drive, turn left along East Green Drive, also signposted to Main Road.
7. At the Main Road turn left, and after a very short distance turn right, signposted to Mary Arden's House.
8. Continue to follow the signposts into Wilmcote and to Mary Arden's house.
9. After visiting the house, continue along the road that led you into Wilmcote, following the signposts to Aston Cantlow.
10. Turn right at the next T-junction, still following the signposts to Aston Cantlow.
11. Continue through Aston Cantlow Village and at the T-junction turn right, signposted to Bearley and Norton Lindsey.
12. Pass under the aqueduct that carries the Stratford-upon-Avon Canal overhead, and then under the main Stratford-upon-Avon to Birmingham railway line before arriving at a crossroads with the main A3400. Go straight on at this crossroads, signposted to Norton Lindsey.
13. Pass through the village of Langley, and after about a mile go right at the T-junction signposted to Wolverton.
14. After just over two more miles, go right again in Wolverton, signposted to Snitterfield.
15. Follow the road through Snitterfield to the crossroads, turn left here and continue up to Snitterfield memorial. Go left at the memorial.
16. After a short distance the road bends right to join the modern, very busy bypass. Go straight ahead where the road bends and you will enter Park Lane and then a pedestrian/cycle pathway which is on the course of the old road and running parallel to

the modern bypass. At the end of this section, the pathway bends right and you must cross the bypass to the pedestrian and cycle shared-use path on the far side. Go left along this path and after a very short distance go right along the much more peaceful Sand Barn Lane, signposted to Hampton Lucy.

17. At the crossroads with the A46, go straight ahead, signposted to Hampton Lucy. Follow this lane to Hampton Lucy.
18. In Hampton Lucy follow the road around through the village and over the bridges signposted to Charlecote. You will see Charlecote Deer Park on your right.
19. At the T-junction in Charlecote, turn right, signposted to Wellesbourne and Stratford-upon-Avon.
20. At the crossroads by Wellesbourne Airfield, go straight ahead, signposted to Loxley.
21. After passing the airfield on your left, you will come to a T-junction, go right, signposted to Loxley.
22. Continue through Loxley village and eventually you will come to a T-junction with the Tiddington Road just outside Stratford-upon-Avon. Go left at this junction.
23. After a short distance you will come to the edge of Stratford-upon-Avon. Go right over the bridge and you will see the theatre on your left.

Nearby

Stratford-upon-Avon is a tourist mecca which is known throughout the world. History is everywhere. Even the information office in Stratford-upon-Avon, situated in Judith Quiney's House in High Street, has historical significance in its own right. Judith Quiney was Shakespeare's younger daughter who married Thomas Quiney.

Another example of a less obvious historical connection can be found just a few doors away from Judith Quiney's house at Harvard House. This was the home of a local butcher's daughter, Katharine Rogers, who married Robert Harvard. Their son, John Harvard, went to America to become the founder of Harvard University (Harvard House is now owned by the university).

Ride 27

The Greenway, Stratford-upon-Avon

A riverside and railway path ride from the Memorial Theatre Gardens, behind the racecourse and out into rolling, leafy Warwickshire.

Maps: Landranger 1:50000 series. Sheet number 151

Distance: 10 miles (16 km) return. Stratford-upon-Avon to Milcote picnic area and back is 6 miles (9.5 km).

Waymarked: The Greenway is easily followed and there are informative boards at main access points.

Gradients: None

Surface: Quiet back streets then two and a half miles on a first class cycleway surface. The next two and a half miles are along a bridleway which can be slippery when wet.

Future Proposals: N/A

Shops and Refreshments: Mainly in Stratford-upon-Avon but also some shops and pubs close to the route

Special Warnings: The Greenway is very popular with walkers, especially close to Stratford-upon-Avon and behind the racecourse, particularly on race days.

Permits: N/A

The Stratford-upon-Avon Greenway follows the line of the disused Stratford-upon-Avon to Cheltenham railway which heads south-south-west out of Stratford-upon-Avon. It cuts across the Milcote estate between Weston-on-Avon and Clifford Chambers, towards Long Marston. The first two and a half miles out of Stratford-upon-Avon are along a well made up cycleway and footpath with an excellent all-weather surface. A mile from Stratford-upon-Avon you are strongly reminded of the Greenway's railway origins as you cross a massive girder bridge which was obviously designed to take the weight of trains rather than just cyclists and walkers.

This line carried such famous trains as The Cornishman Express which thundered its way between the Midlands and the South-West of England. The Milcote picnic area occupies the site of the old Milcote Station and goods yard. You will be able to see where the passenger platforms were, alongside some large pine trees; the goods yard and a signal box were on the other side of the lane.

The line closed for railway traffic in 1976 and is now in local authority ownership. The construction project of the cycleway and footpath, which included the re-decking of the Avon girder bridge, was carried out in 1987/88. There are plenty of good stopping off points with seats, picnic tables and careful tree planting creating a superb recreational environment.

Access Points

The route directions lead from the centre of Stratford-upon-Avon, but you can also start at Milcote Picnic Area or at a convenient car park just on the edge of the town.

The Route

1. From the theatre in the centre of Stratford-upon-Avon, head south, away from the bridge and keeping the river and the gardens on your left.
2. At the T-junction, turn left and follow the road around past Holy Trinity (the Collegiate Church). Just after passing the church, turn left into Mill Lane.
3. At the end of Mill Lane take the pedestrian access towards the river and you will then immediately join the Greenway.
4. Follow the Greenway as it takes you out of the built-up area around Stratford-upon-Avon and passes the race course.
5. At Milcote picnic area the Greenway crosses a lane and continues to Long Marston as a bridleway.
6. When you have reached the end or when you have had enough, turn around and retrace your outward route to return to the centre of Stratford-upon-Avon.

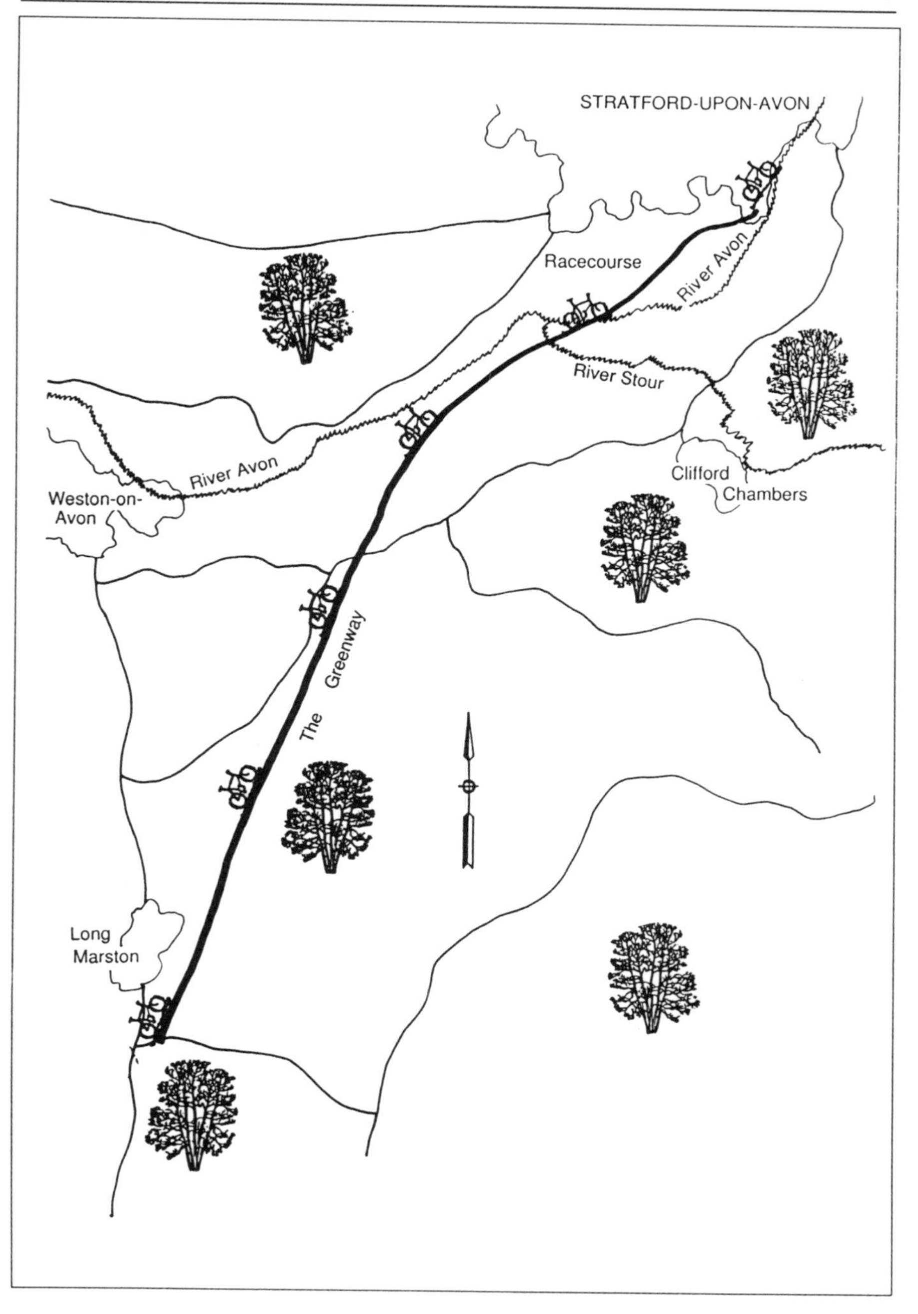
STRATFORD-UPON-AVON
Racecourse
River Avon
River Stour
River Avon
Weston-on-Avon
Clifford Chambers
The Greenway
Long Marston

Nearby

You cannot visit Stratford-upon-Avon without, in one way or another, becoming aware of its Shakespearean connection. A list of the main Shakespearean attractions is available from the Stratford-upon-Avon tourist information offices. The best-known of the attractions within the town are probably Shakespeare's Birthplace in Henley Street, Hall's Croft (his daughter's house) in Old Town, The Royal Shakespeare Theatre in Waterside, The Guildhall (the venue of his first play), the grammar school where he was educated and Nash's House (where his grand-daughter lived).

There is, however, another very important site which is not always included on the main Shakespearean tour itinerary – possibly because the tour buses cannot easily manoeuvre past! We pass this as we cycle out of town towards The Greenway, and it must surely be one of the most important sites for serious Shakespeare aficionados – his burial place in the Collegiate Church of the Holy Trinity.

This lovely, riverside 13th century church is worth a visit under any circumstances. It is approached down a glorious avenue of limes and in the chancel, above his grave and set into a recess in the wall, is a bust of Shakespeare, quill in hand and apparently in deep thought, as if he were planning his next line.

Ride 28

The Birmingham grand tour

A full touring ride around the greater Birmingham area.

Maps: Birmingham A to Z. Landranger 1:50000 series. Mainly sheets 139 and 150, also sheets 127 and 138.

Distance: Total circuit 125 miles (201 km)

If the idea of cycling a circuit around Birmingham sends up images of motorways, main roads, shopping precincts, airports and factory estates, this ride will be one long disappointment. Country lanes, green parks and canal towing-paths are the ingredients used to make up the vast majority of this route. It is carefully thought out to ensure that there is a surprising lack of traffic, some superb rural scenery and plenty of interest to the industrial archaeologist. Lovely country villages offer quiet and peaceful resting places, and where the route skirts into built-up areas, it will take you away from the mainstream and into the far more ordered world of parks, fine suburban roads and canal towing-paths.

With a total distance of 125 miles (201 km), you can spend a couple of days or more on this route or you may wish to ride in sections over a number of weekends. In terms of actual cycling time, an average cyclist should allow about 16 hours non-stop pedalling. Don't forget the trains and how useful they can be in transporting you and your bicycle to and from starting and finishing points.

Access Points

One of the first decisions when planning a circular route is in finding an equitable start/finish point. This route starts its circuit from the centre of the circle. The first leg is from Gas Street Basin to Aldersley Canal Junction, the junction of the BCN canal network and the Staffordshire and Worcester Canal near Wolverhampton. This incorporates the Black Country Cycleway as described in Ride 7. If you prefer to ignore this leg, Autherley Canal Junction (near to Aldersley Canal Junction) makes a very convenient starting place but, as with any circular route, it is easy to begin and end at any convenient point.

The Route

1. From Gas Street Basin follow the Black Country Cycle Way (as described in Ride7).
2. At Aldersley Junction turn left along the Staffordshire and Worcester Canal towards Stourport.
3. If you are starting from Autherley Canal Junction, head south-west (right, if you have your back to the Shropshire Union Canal) and after a short distance you will come to Aldersley Junction.
4. Follow the Staffordshire and Worcester Canal to Stourport on Severn as described in Ride 12.
5. From the canal basin in Stourport on Severn, retrace your route along the canal towing-path to the A4025 bridge. Turn right here along the A4025 to head east.
6. After a very short distance turn left along the B4193 and follow this road to Hartlebury village.
7. Go right in Hartlebury village, following the road to Hartlebury Station.
8. At Hartlebury Station carry straight ahead to the T-junction.
9. Turn right at the T-junction and follow this lane to the junction with the A442 at Cutnall Green.
10. Go straight on over the A442 towards Bryan's Green and follow the road to Elmbridge.
11. Go right in Elmbridge and follow the road under the M5 to Wychbold.
12. Pass through the village of Wychbold and leave it by turning left and following the signposts towards the Stoke Works.
13. After passing back under the railway you see the Worcester and Birmingham Canal on your right. After following it for a while, turn right into Weston Hall Road by The Boat and Railway public house.
14. Cross the canal and follow along this road with the Stoke Works on your left.

15. At the junction with the B4091, go straight ahead at this staggered junction (right/left) into Moorgate Road, signposted to Woodgate and Lower Bentley.
16. After about a mile go left at the T-junction and after a short distance you will once again cross over the Worcester and Birmingham Canal.
17. Shortly after crossing over the canal, go right into Stoke Pound Lane.
18. Follow the road around as it crosses and then re-crosses the Worcester and Birmingham Canal by The Queen's Head public house.
19. Turn right into Copyholt Lane.
20. Continue along Copyholt Lane, following the signposts to Web Heath and Redditch.
21. After about four miles continue straight ahead, following the signposts to Redditch (ignoring the left turn).
22. At the mini roundabout, go right, signposted to Golf Course and Feckenham, and follow the road around to the right at the first bend as it goes into Crumpfields Lane.
23. At the T-junction with Sillins Lane, turn right and then immediately left by The Book Inn public house into Ham Green Lane, signposted to Feckenham and Ham Green.
24. At the next junction turn right, signposted to Feckenham.
25. At the Swansbrook Lane and Astwood Lane T-junction, turn right towards Feckenham.
26. Pass through the very pretty Feckenham village and at the T-junction with the B4090, opposite the Lygon Arms public house, turn left.
27. Follow the B4090 to the junction with the A441 at New End.
28. Cross the A441 to continue along the B4090 to the outskirts of Alcester.
29. Go right to follow the A435 south into Alcester.

30. Leave Alcester to the east along the B4089 towards Great Alne and Little Alne.
31. Turn right in Little Alne, signposted to Bearley and Norton Lindsey.
32. Pass under the aqueduct that carries the Stratford-upon-Avon Canal overhead, and then under the main Stratford-upon-Avon to Birmingham railway line before arriving at a crossroads with the main A3400. Go straight on at this crossroads, signposted to Norton Lindsey.
33. Pass through the village of Langley and follow the road to Norton Lindsey.
34. Turn left at the crossroads into Brittons Lane, signposted to Hatton.
35. At the staggered crossroads with the A4189, go straight on (right and immediately left) into the single track lane.
36. At the T-junction turn right, signposted to Hatton. After a very short distance, just before the motorway bridge, turn left, signposted to Hatton Station.
37. Follow this road and follow signposts to Pinley (ignoring the right turn to Hatton Station).
38. At Pinley Green carry straight on over the crossroads towards Lowsensford.
39. After passing the Fleur-de-Lys public house in Lowsensford, continue straight ahead, signposted to Lapworth and Hockley Heath.
40. After a short distance you will once again cross the M40. Continue along this road to the junction with the B4439.
41. Turn left along the B4439. (If you go right here you will shortly come to The Boot public house.)
42. After a very short distance and after crossing the Grand Union Canal, go right, signposted to Chadwick End, Packwood House and Baddesley Clinton.
43. Follow the road signposted to Packwood House and continue through the grounds.

44. After passing through the grounds of Packwood House, you will arrive in Darley Green. After passing under the railway bridge, keep left here along Bakers Lane towards Dorridge.
45. After a few hundred metres turn left into Blue Lake Road which will take you into the suburb of Knowle and Dorridge.
46. After about one third of a mile, at the next T-junction, with Clyde Road to the left and Knowle Wood Road to the right, turn right along Knowle Wood Road.
47. After another quarter of a mile you will come to a five exit junction. Take the second left into Grove Road towards the small traffic roundabout. You will now pass Dorridge Cricket Club on your left.
48. At the small traffic roundabout carry straight ahead into Widney Road.
49. After another quarter of a mile turn right into Tilehouse Green Lane.
50. After about three quarters of a mile, turn right into Longdon Road and follow this road for just over half a mile into Knowle.
51. At the T-junction with Lodge Road, turn left and after just a few metres you will arrive at a main junction with the A41 opposite The Wilsons Arms public house. Cross over this junction by turning right and then immediately left into Hampton Road.
52. Continue along Hampton Road for nearly two miles to the staggered crossroads. Turn right here into Barston Lane, signposted to Barston.
53. Continue to follow Barston Lane through Barston village and then follow signposts for Berkswell for approximately three miles until you are faced with the junction of the main A452. Before arriving at the A452, turn right into Wootton Green Lane.
54. Follow Wooton Green Lane to the T-junction with the A452 in Balsall Common village.
55. Cross over the A452 by turning right and then almost immediately left into Lavender Hall Lane, signposted to Berkswell. Follow Lavender Hill Lane for the half mile or so into Berkswell.

56. In the village of Berkswell turn left at the junction into Berkswell Road, signposted to Meriden.
57. After about two miles you will arrive in Meriden at the junction with the B4102, with a lovely old duck pond on your right.
58. Go left, signposted to Solihull, Nuneaton and Birmingham, along the B4102 for about half a mile to the Meriden Cross and the Cyclist Memorial.
59. At the small traffic roundabout go right and then immediately left into Maxstoke Lane.
60. After about a third of a mile you will come to the crossover junction with the very busy A45(T). Cross over this junction by passing through the gap in the dual carriageway safety crash barrier and continue along the next section of Maxstoke Lane.
61. After about a quarter of a mile turn right at the T-junction signposted towards Maxstoke.
62. Follow this lane under the M6 and for just over two miles to a T-junction, with Maxstoke Church on your left. Turn right here, signposted to Fillongley.
63. After about a quarter of a mile, just after this road takes a sharp left-hand turn, carry straight ahead into Bentley Lane (an unmarked lane).
64. After about a third of a mile turn left at the T-junction into Fillongley Road, signposted to Shustoke.
65. After a quarter of a mile turn right into an unmarked lane to head north again.
66. After nearly half a mile turn left at the grassy triangle junction.
67. At the next grassy triangle junction keep left, signposted to Church End and Shustoke.
68. After about half a mile turn left up the well-hidden lane heading uphill to your left.
69. After about a mile turn right into Hollyland at the grassy triangle junction. Follow this lane to Shustoke.
70. Upon arriving in the outskirts of Shustoke, turn left at the first junction and then almost immediately left again into Back Lane.

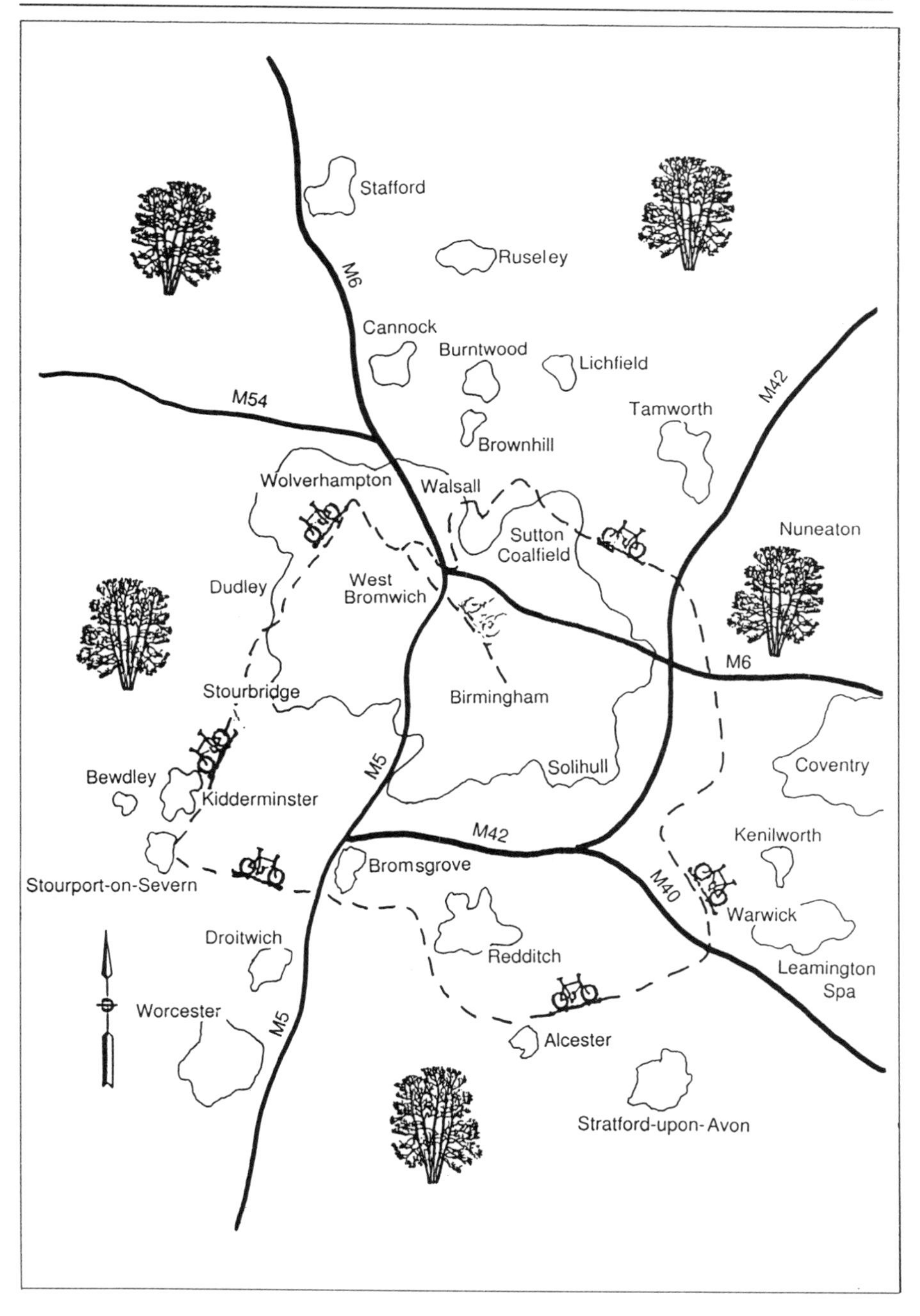
Stafford
Ruseley
M6
Cannock
Burntwood
Lichfield
M54
M42
Tamworth
Brownhill
Wolverhampton
Walsall
Sutton
Coalfield
Nuneaton
Dudley
West
Bromwich
M6
Stourbridge
Birmingham
Coventry
Bewdley
Solihull
M5
Kidderminster
M42
Kenilworth
Stourport-on-Severn
Bromsgrove
M40
Warwick
Droitwich
Redditch
Leamington
Spa
Worcester
M5
Alcester
Stratford-upon-Avon

71. At the end of Back Lane, turn left along the B4114 (Coleshill Road). After passing Shustoke reservoir, turn right along the minor road signposted to Whitacre Heath. Turn right again at the next T-junction.
72. Follow this road for just over two miles – across the railway, through Whitacre Heath, across another railway and past the first lakes of Kingsbury Water Park. You will arrive at a traffic roundabout junction with the A4097.
73. Carry straight ahead over the A4097 for about two miles, past the main entrance to the Kingsbury Water Park, over the M42, over the Birmingham and Fazeley Canal to the junction with the A4091.
74. At the junction with the A4091, just after the football training ground, turn right. After a very short distance, turn left into Brick Kiln Lane, signposted to Hunts Green.
75. At the T-junction turn right, and at the grassy triangle turn left, signposted towards Allen End.
76. Follow this lane for about two miles to the junction of the A446(T).
77. Cross over the A446(T) by turning right and then almost immediately left into Holly Lane, signposted to Walmley.
78. At the end of Holly Lane, after about a mile, turn right, signposted to Sutton Coldfield.
79. Continue straight ahead, following the signposts to Sutton Coldfield. On entering the town, follow the signposts to Sutton Park.
80. Use the tarmac roads in the park to make your way to Streetly Gate, which is in the top north-west corner.
81. Turn right out of Streetly Gate and follow the road to the small traffic roundabout.
82. Take the second exit off the roundabout through the ornate gates and along Roman Road.
83. Follow Roman Road (there are many speed bumps) to the junction with the A454. Go straight over the A454 into Forge Lane, opposite.

84. After about one and half miles turn right at the T-junction signposted to Shenstone.
85. After about one more mile take the left turn into an unsigned lane. After about half a mile you will arrive at a T-junction. Go left here.
86. After another quarter of a mile go right, signposted to Lynn.
87. After another quarter of a mile, keep left at the grassy triangle to go past Stonnall House Farm on your left.
88. At the end of this lane (Mill Lane), turn right into Church Road and then immediately left, signposted to Stonnall and Walsall Wood, into Main Street.
89. Just before reaching the A452, turn right into a continuation of Main Street. At the crossroads with the A452 go straight ahead into Castle Hill Road.
90. Follow Castle Hill Road as it becomes Castle Road to the crossroads of the B4152, Salter's Road. Go straight ahead here into Vigo Road.
91. At the end of Vigo Road you will come to the Daw End Canal. Turn right along the towing-path.
92. After about a mile and a half you will come to the Catshill Junction of the Anglesey Branch Canal. Keep left here to continue west along the Wyrley and Essington Canal.
93. After about two and a half miles you will arrive at Pelsall Junction with the Cannock Extension Canal. Again keep left.
94. Continue for five miles to Birchills Junction. Turn right here to follow the Wyrley and Essington Canal.
95. Follow the Wyrley and Essington Canal for eight miles to Horseley Fields Junction.
96. Turn right at Horseley Fields Junction for Aldersley Junction or turn left at Horseley Fields Junction to return to Gas Street Basin (see Ride 7).